LEISURE ARTS PRESENTS

THE SPIRIT OF CHRISTMAS

CREATIVE HOLIDAY IDEAS BOOK SEVEN

Taking many forms over the centuries, the Christmas gift-bringer is a unique combination of the secular and religious aspects of the season. He is the jolly old man, the kindly bishop, the beloved champion of children. But whether we know him as Father Christmas, St. Nicholas, or Santa Claus, we see him as an embodiment of the spirit of love and sharing that was born on that first Christmas so long ago. His generous character inspires us to give unselfishly to those around us and to spread the age-old message of peace and love. We find great joy in choosing gifts for loved ones, decorating our homes in festive style, and entertaining family and friends. It is our hope that this volume will lead you to discover anew the heartwarming spirit of Christmas.

LEISURE ARTS, INC.
Little Rock, Arkansas

THE SPIRIT OF CHRISTMAS

BOOK SEVEN

''...and it was always said of him, that he knew how to keep Christmas well, if any man alive possessed the knowledge. May that be truly said of us, and all of us!''

— From *A Christmas Carol* by Charles Dickens

EDITORIAL STAFF

Editor-in-Chief: Anne Van Wagner Childs
Executive Director: Sandra Graham Case
Executive Editor: Susan Frantz Wiles
Publications Director: Carla Bentley
Creative Art Director: Gloria Bearden
Production Art Director: Melinda Stout

PRODUCTION
TECHNICAL
Managing Editor: Sherry Taylor O'Connor
Senior Editor: Kathy Rose Bradley
Senior Technical Writer: Ann Brawner Turner
Technical Writers: Chanda English Adams, Candice Treat Murphy, Kimberly J. Smith, and Lynette M. Cook

DESIGN
Design Director: Patricia Wallenfang Sowers
Designers: Diana Heien Suttle, Donna Waldrip Pittard, Linda Diehl Tiano, Rebecca Sunwall Werle, and Mary Lillian Hill
Design Assistant: Kathy Womack Jones

FOODS
Foods Editor: Susan Warren Reeves, R.D.
Assistant Foods Editor: Jane Kenner Prather
Test Kitchen Assistant: Nora Faye Spencer Clift

EDITORIAL
Associate Editor: Dorothy Latimer Johnson
Senior Editor: Linda L. Trimble
Senior Editorial Writer: Laurie S. Rodwell
Advertising and Direct Mail Copywriters: Steven M. Cooper, Marla Shivers, and Tena Kelley Vaughn

ART
Book/Magazine Art Director: Diane M. Ghegan
Senior Production Artist: Michael A. Spigner
Art Production Assistants: Roberta Aulwes, Karen L. Wilson, Kenny L. Gipson, Sonya Cates, M. Katherine Yancey, and Hubrith Esters
Creative Art Assistant: Judith Howington Merritt
Photography Stylists: Karen Smart Hall, Charlisa Erwin Parker, and Christina Tiano
Typesetters: Cindy Lumpkin and Stephanie Cordero
Advertising and Direct Mail Artists: Linda Lovette and Jeff Curtis

BUSINESS STAFF

Publisher: Steve Patterson
Controller: Tom Siebenmorgen
Retail Sales Director: Richard Tignor
Retail Marketing Director: Pam Stebbins
Retail Customer Services Director: Margaret Sweetin
Marketing Manager: Russ Barnett
Executive Director of Marketing and Circulation: Guy A. Crossley
Fulfillment Manager: Byron L. Taylor
Print Production: Nancy Reddick Lister and Laura Lockhart

Library of Congress Catalog Card Number 93-78118
International Standard Book Number 0-942237-22-6

TABLE OF CONTENTS

Page 6

TABLE OF CONTENTS
(Continued)

Page 92

Page 112

INTERNATIONAL SAMPLER DINNERS..... 114

YOU'RE INVITED!....... 122

CHRISTMAS "LIGHTS" 130

THE SIGHTS OF CHRISTMAS

Connecting us to past celebrations, each ornament we bring out at Christmastime holds a special memory. A trinket that belonged to our great-grandparents proclaims our rich family legacy. A cherished keepsake we received at a more recent Yuletide gathering is a reminder of our own family and friends. But the decorations we lovingly prepare each year to grace our home and to trim our tree are included among our favorites, too. A very personal expression of our own joy in the season, each new creation embraces the promise of Christmases to come.

BEARY MERRY ELVES

Clad in colorful clothes, these beary merry elves have teamed up to tackle their holiday duties at Santa's workshop! Under the keen supervision of the Head Elf, they are hard at work putting the finishing touches on this festive tree. Some of the elves are festooning the branches with shiny ribbon garland and cheerful lights; their miniature tote boxes hold lots of tiny tools to aid in their tasks. Other mischievous helpers are spreading multicolor patterns from their whimsical buckets of paint, while the more adventurous elves are using small stepladders to reach every bough on the tree. From the security of a ''playpen'' box, little bears who are too young to help watch the chaotic efforts wistfully, awaiting the day when they too can contribute to the Christmas preparations.

From the bright packages at the bottom to the candy-striped tree topper pointing the way around the North Pole, the elves have created a tree that is sure to receive the approval of Santa and Mrs. Bear Claus. Beside the stairs, a cheerful crazy quilt echoes the comical confusion in the workshop. And on the landing, there's a rocking chair for extra-special bears who deserve a break from all the activity.

This year, why not invite these busy elves to your home to help you prepare for the holidays? They'll make sure you have the merriest Christmas ever! Instructions for the projects begin on page 16.

(Clockwise from top left) The **North Pole Tree Topper** *(page 23)* on the **Beary Merry Tree** *(page 16)* makes it easy for visitors to find their way around Santa's headquarters. Dressed in dapper **Beary Merry Elf-Wear** *(page 16)*, these happy-go-lucky bears are taking orders from the Head Elf. He's making sure that there are plenty of **Toolboxes** *(page 22)* and **Paint Buckets and Brushes** *(page 24)* to go around. Other elves are hard at work stringing lights and garlands. And, of course, all of them are trying to keep their balance!

With wrapping paper and bright ribbon, it's easy to transform your door into a giant gift-wrapped package! The door garland, trimmed with lots of beary merry decorations, will make your holiday callers think they've arrived at the North Pole!

Mixing mischievous elves with "magic" paint leads to madcap mishaps! When these capricious elves aren't using their **Paint Buckets and Brushes** *(page 24)* to paint everything in sight with polka dots, stripes, and other patterns, they're apt to be turning everything else in Santa's workshop topsy-turvy, including themselves!

(Bottom left) Created from fabrics in bold colors and patterns, the **Cuffed Stocking** *(page 24)* and the **Crazy Quilt Stocking** *(page 21)* make merry decorations until Santa Bear Claus arrives to fill them with Christmas treats.

(Bottom right) To check on the progress of their helpers, **Santa and Mrs. Bear Claus** *(page 19)* drop in on the Christmas preparations at the North Pole workshop. We outfitted them in colorful clothes to coordinate with other projects in the collection.

It's nap time for these diaper-clad "elves-in-waiting," although some of these baby bears would rather stay up and play! When Santa's littlest helpers aren't snuggling up in it, the **Crazy Quilt** *(page 21)* makes a cheerful wall hanging.

Your own little helper will look adorable in this cute **"I've Been Good" Apron** *(page 21)*. Handy pockets are perfect for holding crayons or Christmas gift tags. Our child-sized rocker with its **"Good Little Children" Chair Pad** *(page 24)* is just the right spot for a youngster (or an elf!) to take a break from the holiday hustle and bustle.

This baby bear is receiving encouragement from his playmates as he clambers up to join them. Corralling all of Santa's tiniest helpers in one place is a wonderful way to show them off (and keep them out of trouble!) when company comes calling.

These fun-loving elves painted a miniature sleigh in merry Christmas colors to create a fanciful holiday centerpiece. Gaily wrapped packages and greenery fill the sleigh, while **Paint Buckets and Brushes** *(page 24)* are evidence of their handiwork.

The beary merry elves from the "Gift Wrap Department" have commandeered the **Gift Wrapping Tree** *(page 16).* Shiny packages with multicolored bows and oversized gift tags are perched among the branches. Ready with spools of ribbon and rolls of gift paper, these industrious elves can handle packages in any shape and size. Individual Christmas tree light bulbs make imaginative ornaments. From the little chair at the top to the polka-dot tree skirt at its base, this tree has been wrapped in cheery Christmas charm by Santa's energetic helpers!

BEARY MERRY TREE

(Shown on page 8)

Whether you use bears from a personal collection or purchased ones, recreating our cheerful Beary Merry Tree is fun and easy using the instructions included here.

To set the stage for our busy bear elves, the traditional large lights placed on the tree wind around onto the floor, and a chain garland made from loops of ribbon is draped among the branches. To make the elves' jobs easier, 18" high wooden stepladders painted with bright solids, dots, and stripes are placed on and below the tree. The North Pole Tree Topper (page 23) made from foam core board points the way to important locations.

Adorable purchased 8", 12", and 15" jointed teddy bears make up our crew of Beary Merry Elves. Their Beary Merry Elf-Wear (this page) includes hats, collars, aprons, shorts, and boots. The bears are wired into position on the tree ready to work. The Head Elf sitting upon his ladder with whistle in hand supervises the mischievous group.

Foam core board Toolboxes (page 22) filled with toy tools are placed at strategic spots about the tree, and purchased wooden toy saws are also close at hand. Completing the array of decorating equipment are Paint Buckets and Brushes (page 24) that are made with plaster of paris and painted with bold colors and patterns. The paintbrush ornaments are hung with nylon line. A few of the topsy-turvy elves frolic at the foot of the tree among the extra buckets of paint.

GIFT WRAPPING TREE

(Shown on page 15)

On this four-foot-tall tree, a 12" Beary Merry Elf has gathered a group of his fellow 8" elves to help with wrapping all the gifts in Santa's workshop. Standing on a purchased red ladder-back chair, he observes the progress of the work.

Some of the gifts — already wrapped, tied with curling ribbon, and embellished with oversized poster board tags — are tucked among the branches of the tree. Light bulb ornaments made by gluing loops of nylon line to large, brightly-colored bulbs hang between the packages.

While one small elf rests atop the tree in another chair, the other bears hold swirls and curls of ribbon and rolls of gift wrap as they wait for the next group of packages to arrive. Skirting this wrapping affair is a piece of red fabric scattered with multicolored dots.

BEARY MERRY ELF-WEAR (Shown on pages 10, 13, and 15)

Beary Merry Elf-Wear is designed to fit small (8"), medium (12"), and large (15") jointed teddy bears. The following table indicates which clothing instructions are included for each size bear.

Clothing Item	Small Bear	Medium Bear	Large Bear
Hat	•	•	•
Collar		•	
Apron	•	•	•
Shorts		•	
Boots		•	
Diaper	•		

HATS

For hat to fit small, medium, or large bear, you will need the following piece of fleece fabric: a 12" square for small hat, a 16" square for medium hat, or a 10" square for large hat; thread to match fabric; fabric glue; fabric marking pencil; string; and thumbtack or pin.

1. (**Note:** To cut out hat, follow Step 1 for small hat, Step 2 for medium hat, and Step 3 for large hat.) For small hat, press 12" fabric square in half diagonally, unfold, and cut along pressed line; discard 1 half. To mark bottom edge of hat, tie 1 end of string to fabric marking pencil. Insert thumbtack through string 11½" from pencil. Insert thumbtack in 1 corner of fabric as shown in **Fig. 1** and mark cutting line; cut fabric along marked line.

Fig. 1

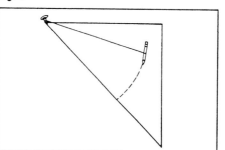

2. For medium hat, repeat Step 1, using 16" fabric square and inserting thumbtack through string 15½" from pencil.
3. For large hat, tie 1 end of string to fabric marking pencil. Insert thumbtack through string 9" from pencil. To mark bottom edge of hat, insert thumbtack in 1 corner of 10" fabric square as shown in **Fig. 2** and mark cutting line; cut fabric along marked line.

Fig. 2

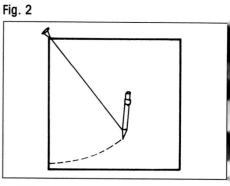

4. With right sides together and matching straight edges, fold hat piece in half. Use a ¼" seam allowance to sew straight edges together. Clip seam allowance at point and press seam open.
5. Press bottom edge of hat ½" to wrong side. Glue in place; allow to dry. Turn hat right side out and press.
6. Place hat on bear and use fabric marking pencil to mark placement of ear openings. Remove hat and cut a slit for each ear opening.

COLLAR

For collar to fit medium bear, you will need one 10½" square of felt, thread to match felt, eight ⅜" gold jingle bells, fabric marking pencil, hot glue gun, glue sticks, and tracing paper.

1. Trace collar pattern, page 18, onto tracing paper; cut out.
2. Fold felt square in half from top to bottom and again from left to right. Matching dotted lines of pattern to folds of felt, place pattern on felt. Use fabric marking pencil to draw around pattern. Cutting through all layers, cut out collar along solid lines only. For opening in back of collar, cut through 1 thickness of fabric along 1 fold from outer to inner edge. Unfold collar.
3. Glue 1 bell to each collar point.
4. Place collar on bear; tack in place.

APRONS

For apron to fit small, medium, or large bear, you will need the following piece of reversible fabric: a 6½" square for small apron, a 7½" square for medium apron, or an 11½" square for large apron; ½"w single-fold bias tape; thread to match fabric and bias tape; paint pen with fine point for large apron (optional); tracing paper; and fabric marking pencil.

Note: Measurements for small apron are given in instructions with measurements for medium and large aprons in parentheses.

1. For small or medium apron, trace desired apron pattern, page 18, onto tracing paper; cut out. For large apron, trace apron pattern, page 18, onto tracing paper, extending bottom of pattern 2"; cut out.
2. Fold fabric square in half. Matching dotted line of pattern to fold of fabric, place pattern on fabric. Use fabric marking pencil to draw around pattern. Cutting through both layers, cut out apron along solid lines only; unfold.
3. For binding, cut the following lengths of bias tape: a 5½" (6¼", 8") length for pocket, a 2¼" (2½", 3¾") length for top of apron, and two 16" (21", 26") lengths for ties. Matching wrong sides, press each length of bias tape in half lengthwise.
4. (**Note:** Refer to photo for remaining steps.) For pocket, insert bottom edge of apron into fold of pocket binding length; stitch in place. Press bottom edge of apron 1¼" (2", 3") to 1 side (right side). To divide pocket, stitch from center bottom of apron to center top of pocket.
5. Insert top edge of apron into fold of apron top binding length; stitch in place.
6. Press each side edge of apron ¼" to wrong side; stitch in place.
7. For each tie, center 1 curved raw edge of apron in fold of one 16" (21", 26") length of binding. Stitching from 1 end of binding to the other, stitch all layers together close to inner edge of binding.
8. If desired, use paint pen to write "Head Elf" on large apron; allow to dry.

SHORTS

For shorts to fit medium bear, you will need two 5½" x 11½" pieces and one 1½" x 20" strip of fabric, 20" of ⅜"w ribbon, thread to match fabric and ribbon, 2 buttons (optional), 10" of ½"w elastic, seam ripper, tracing paper, and fabric marking pencil.

1. Trace cutout pattern, page 19, onto tracing paper; cut out.
2. Matching short edges, fold one 5½" x 11½" fabric piece in half. Referring to **Fig. 1**, place cutout pattern on folded fabric piece. Use fabric marking pencil to draw around pattern. Cutting

through both layers, cut along drawn line; discard cutouts and unfold fabric piece. Using fabric piece as a pattern, cut out remaining 5½" x 11½" fabric piece.

Fig. 1

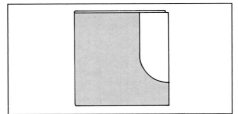

3. (**Note:** Use a ¼" seam allowance unless otherwise indicated.) Matching edges, place fabric pieces right sides together. Referring to **Fig. 2**, sew fabric pieces together along each curved edge (for center seams). Clip seam allowances at curves and press open.

Fig. 2

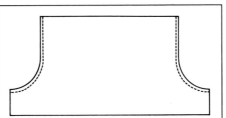

4. For hem, press each bottom raw edge ¼" to wrong side; press ¼" to wrong side again and stitch in place.
5. Matching center seams of shorts, sew inseams (**Fig. 3**).

Fig. 3

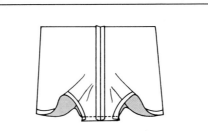

6. For elastic casing at waist, press top edge of shorts ¼" to wrong side; press ¾" to wrong side again. Stitch ⅝" from top edge of pants.
7. Use seam ripper to open casing on inside of pants at 1 seamline. Thread elastic through casing. Overlap ends of elastic ½" and stitch securely together. Sew casing closed. Turn shorts right side out and press.

8. For suspenders, press each long edge of fabric strip ⅜" to wrong side. Center ribbon right side up on strip, covering raw edges of fabric. Sew along each long edge of ribbon to secure. Cut two 8" lengths and one 4" length from strip. Referring to **Fig. 4**, tack suspender pieces together.

Fig. 4

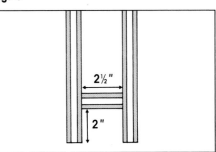

9. Place shorts on bear. Referring to photo, place suspenders on bear, tucking ends of suspenders into shorts. Tack ends of suspenders in place. If desired, sew buttons to shorts below suspender straps.

BOOTS

For boots to fit medium bear, you will need two 6" x 12" pieces of fleece fabric, thread to match fabric, two ½ yd lengths of ½"w satin ribbon, polyester fiberfill, tracing paper, fabric marking pencil, and fabric glue.

1. Trace boot pattern, page 19, onto tracing paper; cut out.
2. (**Note:** Follow Steps 2 - 5 for each boot.) Matching right sides and short edges, fold 1 fabric piece in half. With dotted line of pattern along fold, place pattern on fabric piece. Use fabric marking pencil to draw around pattern. Cutting through both layers, cut out boot along solid lines only; do not unfold.
3. Leaving top edge open, use a ¼" seam allowance to sew remaining raw edges of boot together. Trim seam allowance to ⅛".
4. Fold top edge of boot ¾" to wrong side. Glue in place; allow to dry. Turn boot right side out and press.
5. Stuff toe of boot with fiberfill. Place boot on bear. Referring to photo, tie 1 ribbon length into a bow around top of boot.

Continued on page 18

DIAPER

For diaper to fit small bear, you will need a 9½" square of white fabric cut with pinking shears and a 3" kilt pin (available at fabric stores).

Fold fabric in half diagonally. Referring to photo, place diaper on bear. Secure with pin.

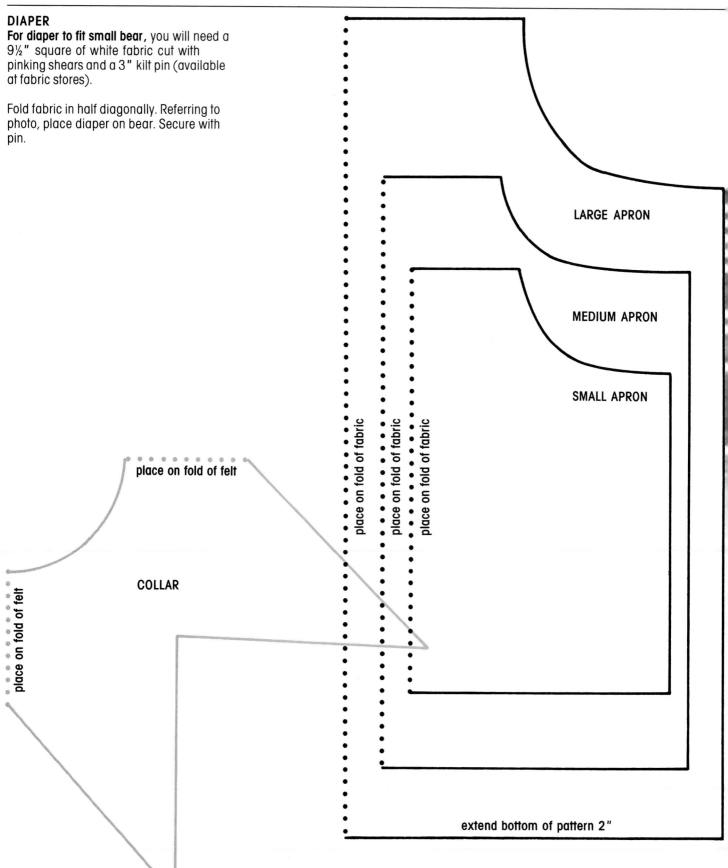

LARGE APRON

MEDIUM APRON

SMALL APRON

place on fold of fabric

place on fold of fabric

place on fold of fabric

place on fold of felt

COLLAR

place on fold of felt

extend bottom of pattern 2"

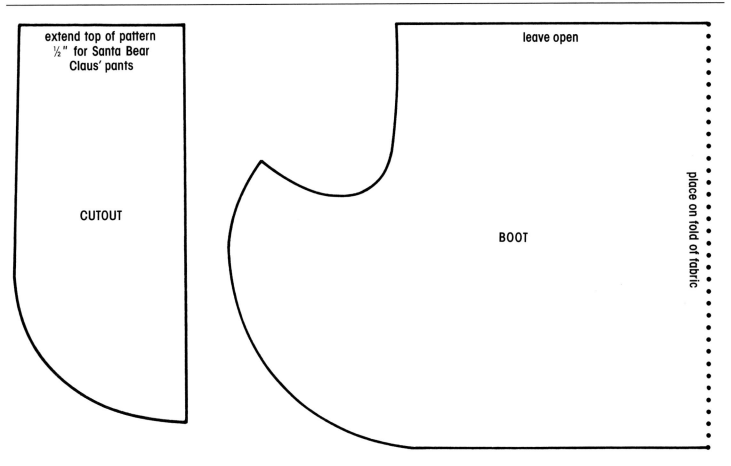

extend top of pattern ½" for Santa Bear Claus' pants

CUTOUT

leave open

BOOT

place on fold of fabric

SANTA AND MRS. BEAR CLAUS (Shown on page 12)

You will need two 15" jointed teddy bears, thread to match fabrics, tracing paper, and fabric marking pencil.

For Santa Bear Claus, you will also need the following fabric pieces: two 7" x 11½" pieces and two 7¾" x 10½" pieces for shirt, two 6¾" x 12" pieces for pants, one 8" x 20" piece for vest, and one 10" square for hat; one 3" x 14½" strip and two 2½" x 12" strips of artificial lamb fleece for trim on hat and pants; two 3½" lengths and one 7½" length of ⅛"w elastic; 14½" of ½"w elastic; ½"w single-fold bias tape for vest binding; ½"w single-fold bias tape for vest pockets; white thread and thread to match bias tape; 1½" white pom-pom; three ⅜" jingle bells; heavyweight non-fusible interfacing; seam ripper; string; thumbtack or pin; craft glue; white curly doll hair; and 3½"w black wire doll glasses.

For Mrs. Bear Claus, you will also need the following fabric pieces: two 11½" x 13" pieces and two 8" x 10" pieces for dress, one 6¾" x 18" piece for apron skirt, one 2" x 30½" strip of fabric for apron waistband and ties, one 3½" x 5" piece

for apron bib, and one 9½" dia. circle for cap; 25½" of 1¼"w white eyelet trim for dress; 33" of ⅛"w ribbon for dress; 32" of ⅜"w lace trim for hat; two 4½" lengths and one 28" length of ⅛"w elastic; two ½" dia. buttons for apron; grey curly doll hair; and 2⅝"w gold wire doll glasses.

Note: For all sewing steps, match right sides and raw edges and pin fabric pieces together. Use a ¼" seam allowance unless otherwise indicated. Cut corners diagonally and clip seam allowances at curves.

SANTA BEAR CLAUS
1. For shirt, trace cutout pattern, this page, onto tracing paper; cut out.
2. Use 7" x 11½" fabric pieces and follow Step 2 of Shorts instructions (Beary Merry Elf-Wear), page 17. For sleeves, use 7¾" x 10½" fabric pieces and repeat.
3. To assemble shirt, refer to **Fig. 1** and sew 1 curved edge of 1 sleeve piece to 1 curved edge of 1 shirt piece; sew 1 curved edge of remaining sleeve piece to remaining curved edge of same shirt

piece. Repeat to sew remaining curved edges of sleeve pieces to curved edges of second shirt piece. Press seams open.

Fig. 1

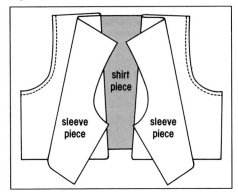

4. Matching front and back of shirt, press shirt flat. Sew side and underarm seams.
5. For casing at bottom of each sleeve, press raw edge ¼" to wrong side; press ½" to wrong side again. Stitch ⅜" from bottom edge of sleeve. Use seam ripper to open casing on inside of sleeve at seamline. Thread one 3½" length of

Continued on page 20

elastic through casing. Overlap ends of elastic ½" and stitch securely together. Sew casing closed.

6. For casing at neck, repeat Step 5, using 7½" length of elastic.

7. For hem, press bottom edge of shirt ¼" to wrong side; press ¼" to wrong side again and stitch in place.

8. For pants, trace cutout pattern, page 19, onto tracing paper, extending top of pattern ½"; cut out.

9. Use 6¾" x 12" fabric pieces and extended cutout pattern and follow Steps 2 and 3 of Shorts instructions, page 17.

10. For pants trim, match wrong sides and fold each 2½" x 12" strip of fleece in half lengthwise. For each trim piece, match long raw edge of trim piece to 1 bottom raw edge of pants and pin trim piece on right side of pants. Sew trim to pants along long raw edge. Fold trim down and press seam allowance toward pants.

11. To complete pants, follow Steps 5 - 7 of Shorts instructions, page 17, using 14½" length of elastic.

12. For vest, trace vest pattern, page 21, onto tracing paper and cut out.

13. Match short edges and fold vest fabric piece in half. With dotted line of pattern along fold, place pattern on fabric piece. Use fabric marking pencil to draw around pattern. Cutting through both layers, cut out vest along solid lines only; unfold.

14. For binding, cut one 31½", one 4½", and two 10¼" lengths of bias tape. Matching wrong sides, press each length of bias tape in half lengthwise.

15. To bind front opening and bottom edges, insert raw edge of vest into fold of 31½" length of binding. Stitch in place.

16. To bind neck and armhole edges, repeat Step 15, using 4½" length of binding for neck edge and 10¼" lengths of binding for armhole edges.

17. Sew shoulder seams. Turn right side out and press.

18. For each vest pocket, cut a 1⅝" length of bias tape; press ends ⅛" to wrong side. Referring to photo for placement, place pocket on vest; stitch in place close to bottom and side edges of pocket.

19. For buttons, sew jingle bells to vest.

20. For hat, follow Steps 3 and 4 of Hats instructions (Beary Merry Elf-Wear), page 16.

21. For hat trim, match short edges and fold 3" x 14½" strip of fleece in half; sew short edges together to form a loop. Finger press seam open. Matching wrong sides and raw edges, fold trim in half. Stitching very close to raw edges, use a

medium width zigzag stitch with a medium stitch length to sew long edges together. Matching zigzagged edge of trim piece to bottom edge of hat and matching seams, pin trim piece on right side of hat. Stitch in place. Fold trim down and finger press seam allowance toward hat. Turn hat right side out and press. Tack pom-pom to point of hat.

22. Place hat on bear. Use fabric marking pencil to mark placement of ears on seamline at top of trim. Remove hat. Use seam ripper to remove stitching along seamline for ear openings.

23. For beard, cut a beard shape from interfacing to fit bear. Glue doll hair to interfacing, covering shape. Allow to dry.

24. Place shirt, pants, vest, and hat on bear. Tuck a small amount of doll hair under front edge of hat. Place glasses on bear. Tack beard to bear.

MRS. BEAR CLAUS

1. For dress, trace cutout pattern, page 19, onto tracing paper; cut out.

2. Matching long edges, use 11½" x 13" fabric pieces and follow Step 2 of Shorts instructions (Beary Merry Elf-Wear), page 17. For sleeves, use 8" x 10" fabric pieces and follow Step 2 of Shorts instructions.

3. To assemble dress, follow Step 3 of Santa Bear Claus instructions, page 19.

4. To hem each sleeve, press bottom edge ¼" to wrong side; press ¼" to wrong side again and stitch in place.

5. To gather each sleeve, place one 4½" length of elastic on wrong side of sleeve; securely machine tack 1 end of elastic in place at 1 raw edge of sleeve (**Fig. 1**). Stretching elastic as you sew, use a medium width zigzag stitch with a medium stitch length and stitch over elastic, being careful not to catch elastic in stitching; securely machine tack remaining end of elastic in place at opposite edge of sleeve.

Fig. 1

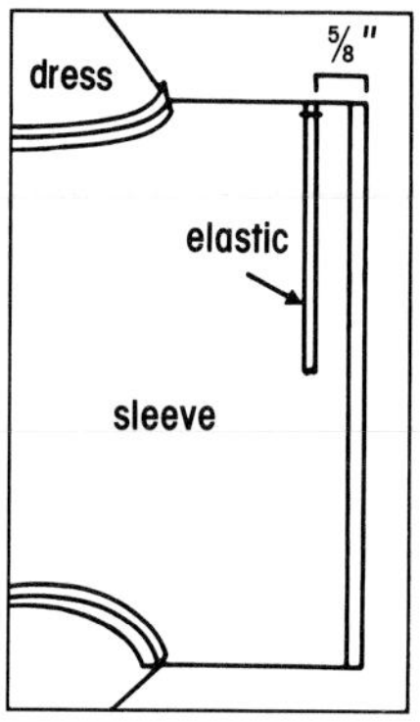

dress

elastic

sleeve

6. Matching front and back of dress, press dress flat. Sew side and underarm seams.

7. For casing at neck, press raw edge ¼" to wrong side; press ½" to wrong side again. Stitch ⅜" from top edge of neck.

8. For eyelet trim, begin at center back of dress and match right side of trim to wrong side of dress, overlapping raw edge of trim ¼" over neck edge of dress; pin in place. Stitching very close to neck edge of dress, sew trim to dress.

9. At center back of dress, cut a small opening on inside of casing. Thread ribbon through casing.

10. To hem dress, press bottom edge ¼" to wrong side; press ½" to wrong side again and stitch in place.

11. Turn dress right side out and press.

12. For apron skirt, press each short edge of skirt fabric piece ¼" to wrong side; press ¼" to wrong side again and stitch in place.

13. Press 1 raw edge (bottom) of skirt ¼" to wrong side; press 1" to wrong side again and stitch in place.

14. To gather skirt, baste ⅜" and ¼" from remaining raw edge. Pull basting threads, drawing up gathers to 9".

15. For apron waistband and ties, press all edges of fabric strip ½" to wrong side; with wrong sides together, press strip in half lengthwise. Center gathered edge of skirt in fold of strip; pin in place. Stitching from 1 end of fabric strip to the other, stitch all layers together close to pressed edges of strip.

16. For bib, match short edges of bib fabric piece and press in half (pressed edge is top). Sew side edges together. Turn right side out and press.

17. With waistband overlapping raw edge of bib ¾", center bib under waistband; pin in place. Refer to **Fig. 2** to sew bib to waistband.

Fig. 2

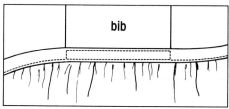

bib

18. Place dress on bear, pulling ribbon ends to gather casing at neck; tie ends into a bow. Tie apron around bear and pin bib to dress. Mark bib placement with fabric marking pencil. Remove dress from bear. Stitching through bib and dress, sew buttons to top corners of bib.

SANTA AND MRS. BEAR CLAUS (continued)

19. For cap, place lace trim right side up on right side of cap fabric circle with straight edge of lace overlapping edge of circle ⅛". Use a narrow width zigzag stitch with a short stitch length to sew lace in place.
20. Pin 28" length of elastic to wrong side of cap 1" inside outer edge of lace.
21. Using a medium width zigzag stitch with a medium stitch length, sew over elastic, being careful not to catch elastic in stitching. Place cap on bear and pull ends of elastic, drawing up gathers to fit. Remove cap. Overlap elastic near cap; tack securely together. Trim excess elastic.
22. Place dress, cap, and glasses on bear. Tuck a small amount of doll hair under front edge of cap.

"I'VE BEEN GOOD" APRON
(Shown on page 13)

You will need a child's canvas apron with binding along edges, fabric for crayon pocket (see Step 1 for amount), thread to match fabric, paint pen with fine point, fabric marking pencil, and jumbo crayons.

1. For crayon pocket, cut a 6" wide piece of fabric same length as width of apron.
2. Press 1 long edge (top) of fabric ¼" to wrong side; press ¾" to wrong side again and stitch in place.
3. Place pocket fabric right side down on a flat surface. Matching bottom edge of apron to long raw edge of fabric, place apron right side down on fabric. Use fabric marking pencil to draw around bottom and side edges of apron on fabric. Cut along drawn line.
4. Measure width of apron binding. Press raw edges of pocket fabric to wrong side the determined measurement.
5. Place pocket fabric right side up on right side of apron, matching pressed edge of fabric to inner edge of apron binding. Stitching close to pressed edge, sew fabric to apron.
6. To divide crayon pocket, refer to photo and sew desired number of evenly spaced lines from apron binding to top of pocket.
7. Refer to photo and use paint pen to write "I've Been Good" on apron. Allow to dry.
8. Place crayons in pockets.

CRAZY QUILT STOCKING
(Shown on page 12)

You will need fabric scraps for quilt block, one 12" x 20" piece of muslin fabric for quilt block backing, one 12" x 20" fabric piece for stocking back, two 12" x 20" fabric pieces for lining, one 2" x 16¼" bias strip of fabric for binding, one 2" x 8" fabric strip for hanger, thread to match fabrics, tracing paper, and fabric marking pencil.

1. For stocking front, use 12" x 20" muslin piece for quilt block backing and follow Steps 1 - 4 of Crazy Quilt instructions, this page, to make 1 quilt block.
2. Follow Steps 1 and 2 of Cuffed Stocking instructions, page 24, to make stocking from stocking front, stocking back, and lining fabric pieces.
3. For binding and hanger, follow Steps 5 - 7 of Cuffed Stocking instructions, page 24.

CRAZY QUILT
(Shown on page 9)

For an approx. 50" square quilt, you will need fabric scraps for quilt blocks, four 25" squares of muslin fabric for quilt block backing, one 50" square of muslin fabric for quilt backing (pieced as necessary), purchased quilt binding, off-white thread, and thread to match binding.

1. (**Note:** Follow Steps 1 - 5 to make 4 quilt blocks. Refer to photo for all steps.) Cut 1 fabric scrap with straight edges. Place scrap right side up at center of 1 quilt block backing piece. Cut a second scrap with 1 edge same length as 1 edge of first scrap.
2. Trim second scrap so that once second scrap is sewn down, pieced area will have no "inside" angles (**Fig. 1**). With right sides facing and matching edges of same length, lay second scrap on first scrap. Using a ¼" seam allowance and sewing through all 3 layers, sew scraps together along matched edge. Press second scrap right side up.

Fig. 1

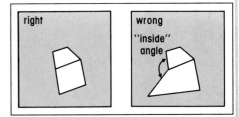

3. Cut a third scrap with 1 edge same length as 1 edge of pieced area. Repeat Step 2 for third scrap.
4. Repeat Step 3, adding scraps until entire quilt block backing piece is covered.
5. If necessary, trim scrap fabric edges even with edges of quilt block backing. Baste ¼" from edges of quilt block.
6. To assemble quilt top, match right sides and raw edges and use a ½" seam allowance to sew quilt blocks together, forming a square. Press seams open.
7. Place quilt top right side up on quilt backing; pin in place. Machine stitch along seamlines between quilt blocks.
8. For binding, open 1 end of binding and press ½" to wrong side; refold. Beginning with unpressed end, insert raw edges of quilt into fold of binding, mitering binding at corners; baste in place. Stitching close to inner edge of binding, sew binding to quilt.

TOOLBOXES (Shown on page 10)

For each toolbox, you will need a 10" x 20" piece of ¼" thick white foam core board, Design Master® glossy red spray paint (available at craft stores or florist shops), green acrylic paint, small paintbrush, 1¼"w x 7¼"l piece of 1" thick plastic foam, white paper, tracing paper, craft knife, cutting mat or thick layer of newspapers, craft glue, hot glue gun, glue sticks, and toy tools.

1. For handle and side patterns, follow **Tracing Patterns**, page 158.
2. Use patterns to draw indicated number of pieces on foam board. Use craft knife to cut out pieces. Cut two 2½" x 3½" pieces for ends and one 3½" x 7½" piece for bottom from foam board.

3. (**Note:** Refer to photo for remaining steps. Use hot glue for each glue step unless otherwise indicated.) To assemble toolbox, lay bottom piece flat. Referring to **Fig. 1**, glue bottom of handle piece along center of bottom piece. Glue end pieces, then side pieces, in place.

Fig. 1

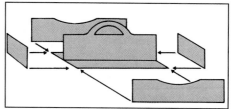

4. Glue plastic foam into bottom of 1 side (front) of toolbox.
5. Allowing to dry between coats, spray paint toolbox red.
6. For letters on toolbox, trace "Tools" pattern onto white paper. Paint stripes in letters green; allow to dry. Cut out letters. Use craft glue to glue letters to front of toolbox; allow to dry.
7. Place tools in box, pressing tools into plastic foam and gluing to secure if necessary.

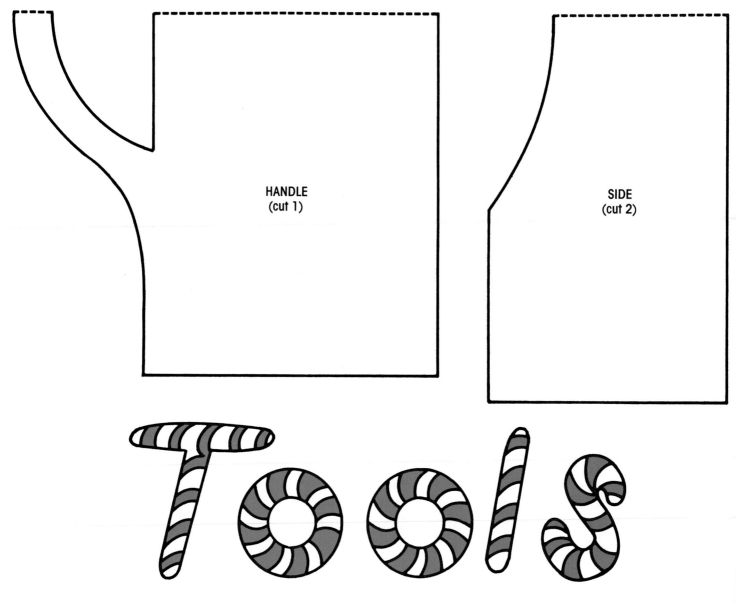

HANDLE
(cut 1)

SIDE
(cut 2)

You will need a 14" x 16" piece of ¼" thick white foam core board, 30" of ½" dia. wooden dowel, 1¼" dia. bead to fit end of dowel, Design Master® glossy red spray paint (available at craft stores or florist shops), white and green acrylic paint, small paintbrushes, craft knife, cutting mat or thick layer of newspapers, red paint pen with fine point, white paper, craft glue, florist wire, hot glue gun, and glue sticks.

1. (**Note:** Refer to photo for all steps. Use craft knife to cut foam board.) Cut one 5½" x 16" piece and three 2" x 12" pieces from foam board.
2. For North Pole sign, cut jagged edges across each end of large foam board piece. For each small sign, cut a point at 1 end of 1 small piece of foam board; cut jagged edges across remaining end.
3. Spray paint North Pole sign and dowel red. Paint bead white. Allow to dry.
4. For letters on North Pole sign, trace "North Pole" pattern onto white paper. Paint stripes in letters green; allow to dry. Cut out letters. Use craft glue to glue letters to sign; allow to dry.
5. For small signs, use paint pen to write "Elf Tool Shed," "Reindeer Barn," and "Toy Work Shop" on signs; allow to dry.
6. Hot glue bead to 1 end of dowel; hot glue signs to dowel.
7. Wire tree topper to top of tree.

"GOOD LITTLE CHILDREN" CHAIR PAD

(Shown on page 13)

You will need fabric for pad (see Step 1 for amount), fabric for ruffle (see Step 3 for amount), thread to match fabrics, 1⅔ yds of ¼"w grosgrain ribbon, medium weight fusible interfacing, polyester fiberfill, and a paint pen with fine point.

1. For pad, cut a piece of interfacing desired finished pad size. Cut 2 fabric pieces ½" larger on all sides than interfacing.
2. For pad front, follow manufacturer's instructions to fuse interfacing to center on wrong side of 1 fabric piece. Refer to photo and use paint pen to write "Good Little Children" on right side of fabric square within interfaced area. Allow to dry.
3. For ruffle, measure top and each side edge of pad front; multiply total by 2½. Cut a strip of fabric 3¾" wide by the determined measurement (pieced as necessary). Press ends of strip ½" to wrong side. With wrong sides together, press strip in half lengthwise.
4. To gather ruffle, baste ⅜" and ¼" from raw edge. Pull basting threads, drawing up gathers to fit top and side edges of pad front.
5. Beginning ½" from bottom on each side edge of pad front and matching raw edges, baste ruffle to right side of pad front (**Fig. 1**).

Fig. 1

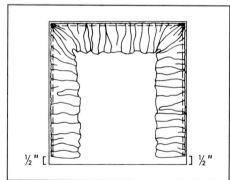

6. Place pad fabric squares right sides together. Using a ½" seam allowance and leaving an opening for turning at bottom of pad, sew squares together, being careful not to catch ends of ruffle in bottom seam of pad.
7. Cut corners diagonally, turn right side out, and press. Lightly stuff pad with fiberfill. Sew final closure by hand.
8. For ties, cut ribbon into 4 lengths. Tack center of 1 length at each corner on back of chair pad.

PAINT BUCKETS AND BRUSHES

(Shown on pages 10 and 14)

You will need desired size metal buckets and paintbrushes (available at craft or paint stores), plaster of paris, a large disposable container for mixing plaster of paris, craft sticks, desired colors of acrylic paint, small paintbrushes for painting, matte clear acrylic spray, glossy clear acrylic spray, and aluminum foil.

PAINT BUCKETS

1. (**Note:** Protect work surface with aluminum foil.) Allowing to dry between coats, apply 2 coats of matte acrylic spray to each bucket.
2. (**Note:** Refer to photo for remaining steps.) For each bucket, loosely crumple aluminum foil into balls. Fill bucket to desired "paint" level with crumpled foil. If desired, place paintbrush in bucket with handle extending above rim.
3. Follow manufacturer's instructions to mix plaster of paris.
4. Pour plaster into each bucket, covering crumpled foil. For each bucket with "paint" pouring out, allow plaster to set slightly, then turn bucket on its side so that plaster pours onto foil as desired; if necessary, shake bucket slightly and use craft stick to spread plaster as desired. Allow to dry.
5. Paint dots, swirls, ripples, and stripes on plaster, leaving no areas unpainted; if desired, paint areas of bucket to resemble paint drips. Allow to dry.
6. Allowing to dry between coats, apply 2 coats of glossy acrylic spray to plaster.

PAINTBRUSHES

1. Follow Steps 1 and 3 of Paint Buckets instructions to prepare paintbrushes and plaster of paris.
2. (**Note:** Refer to photo for remaining steps.) For each paintbrush, dip brush bristles into plaster. If desired, use craft stick to spread plaster from bristles toward handle to resemble drips of paint. Lay paintbrush on foil, prop upright, or hang to dry.
3. Follow Steps 5 and 6 of Paint Buckets instructions to paint and seal plaster.

CUFFED STOCKING

(Shown on page 12)

You will need two 12" x 20" fabric pieces for stocking, two 12" x 20" fabric pieces for lining, one 7" x 19" piece of felt for cuff, one 2" x 16¼" bias strip of fabric for binding, one 2" x 8" fabric strip for hanger, thread to match fabrics and felt, six ⅝" jingle bells, tracing paper, fabric marking pencil, hot glue gun, and glue sticks.

1. Matching registration marks (⊕) and overlapping pattern pieces, trace stocking pattern, page 25, onto tracing paper; cut out.
2. Leaving top edge of stocking open, use pattern and follow **Sewing Shapes**, page 158, to make stocking from stocking fabric pieces; press. Repeat to make lining from lining fabric pieces; do not turn lining right side out. Matching wrong sides, insert lining into stocking; baste top edges together.
3. For cuff pattern, follow **Tracing Patterns**, page 158. Use pattern to cut 1 cuff piece from felt.
4. For cuff, match ends and fold cuff piece in half. Use a ⅜" seam allowance to sew ends together; press seam open. Turn right side out. With wrong side of cuff facing right side of stocking, place cuff over stocking, matching cuff seamline to heel-side seamline of stocking; baste in place.
5. For binding, match wrong sides and press 16¼" bias strip in half lengthwise; unfold. Press long raw edges to center; refold binding. Unfold 1 end of binding and press end ½" to wrong side; refold binding.
6. Beginning with unpressed end of binding at center back of stocking, insert top edges of stocking into fold of binding. Stitching close to inner edge of binding, sew binding to stocking.
7. For hanger, press all edges of 8" fabric strip ½" to wrong side. With wrong sides together, press strip in half lengthwise; sew close to pressed edges. Matching ends, fold hanger in half to form a loop. Place ends of loop inside stocking at heel-side seamline with approx. 2½" of loop extending above stocking; tack in place.
8. Glue 1 jingle bell to each cuff point.

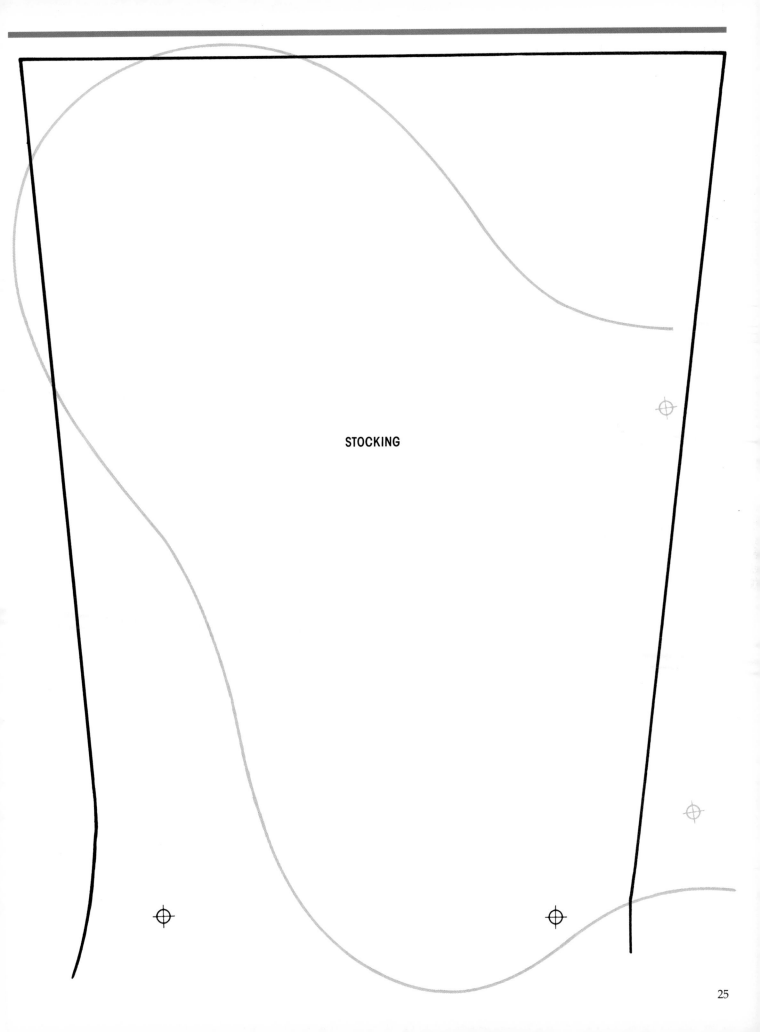

STOCKING

A SLICE OF COUNTRY CHEER

The festive red-and-green color combination of ripe watermelons growing on the vine prompted us to create this country Christmas collection. Seed packet plant pokes and Santa gourd ornaments join the watermelons scattered among the branches of the tree, along with bows made from wired ribbon that you craft yourself. Ready to sprinkle the garden below with a refreshing shower, a decorated watering can makes a cute tree topper. Painted to resemble a slice of the juicy fruit, the tree skirt is edged with striped ticking fabric to coordinate with the jaunty bows. Beneath the tree, a small crate and a little wagon filled with papier mâché melons enhance the farm-fresh flavor. Add a slice of country cheer to your Yuletide celebration with this homegrown collection! Instructions for the projects begin on page 30.

Adorned with decorations from the tree, this cheery wreath makes an adorable addition to door or window. *Opposite*: Trimmings for the **Country Cheer Tree** (*page 30*) include **Santa Ornaments** (*page 34*), **Seed Packet Ornaments** (*page 35*), **Papier Mâché Melons** (*page 31*), and **Wagon Ornaments** (*page 30*). A **Watermelon Vine Garland** (*page 32*) twines around the tree, and **Wired Ribbon Bows** (*page 31*) add country flair. Filled with handcrafted melons, a plant poke, and excelsior, the small wooden **Watermelon Wagon** (*page 30*) beside the tree echoes the little wagon ornaments on the boughs above it.

Gourd Candle Holders (*page 34*) can be grouped together to create a charming table centerpiece. The cute **Place Mats and Napkins** (*page 33*) are sure to delight holiday guests. *Opposite*: The painted canvas **Watermelon Tree Skirt** (*page 31*) looks good enough to eat! Decorations from the tree add a homespun touch to Christmas packages.

COUNTRY CHEER TREE

(Shown on page 27)

Bring a country garden into your home and add a touch of farm-fresh goodness to your Christmas celebration with this refreshing seven-foot-tall tree.

Twining among the branches is our Watermelon Vine Garland (page 32) made from twisted paper wire. The garland's juicy watermelon slices made from painted canvas fabric look good enough to eat. Near the vine, all shapes and sizes of Papier Mâché Melons (page 31) are ready for picking.

Carrying a tiny harvest of watermelons are cute Wagon Ornaments (this page) made from jumbo craft sticks. Painted miniature ornamental gourds make precious Santa Ornaments (page 34). If gourds are not readily available, we've also given instructions for making these gourd shapes using papier mâché.

To mark our rows, perky Seed Packet Ornaments (page 35) are easily made with photocopies and colored pens. Pillow ticking fabric made into Wired Ribbon Bows (page 31) adds a crisp, country look to the garden scene.

A metal watering can at the top of the tree, painted to match the watermelons and tied with its own bow, is ready to provide a fresh shower for our growing crop.

The juicy Watermelon Tree Skirt (page 31) made from painted canvas and trimmed with a bias strip of cheerful ticking fabric completes the garden-fresh decorations.

WAGON ORNAMENTS (Shown on page 28)

For each ornament, you will need 18 jumbo craft sticks; four 1½" dia. wooden wheels; four 1⅜" long wooden axle pegs to fit wheels; 1¼" to 1½" long wooden eggs for watermelons; 7" of ¼" dia. cotton cord; white, red, light green, and green acrylic paint; small flat and liner paintbrushes; one ¼" x ¾" strip of cellulose sponge; black permanent felt-tip pen with fine point; wood excelsior; utility scissors; hot glue gun; and glue sticks.

1. (**Note:** Use utility scissors to cut craft sticks.) For bottom of wagon, cut four 4½" lengths for slats and two 3" lengths for braces from craft sticks. Referring to **Fig. 1**, place slats side by side; glue 1 brace across slats ¼" from each end.

Fig. 1

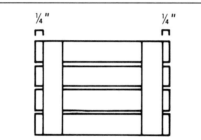

2. For each long side of wagon, cut two 4½" lengths for slats and two 1¼" lengths for braces from craft sticks. Refer to **Fig. 2** and place slats side by side; center and glue 1 brace across slats ¼" from each end.

Fig. 2

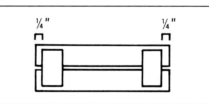

3. For each end of wagon, repeat Step 2, cutting two 3⅛" lengths for slats and two 1¼" lengths for braces from craft sticks.
4. (**Note:** Refer to photo for remaining steps.) With braces facing inside of wagon, glue sides of wagon to bottom; glue ends of wagon to bottom and sides.

5. Use pen to draw dots on ends of wagon slats to resemble nails.
6. (**Note:** Allow to dry after each paint color.) For each wheel, use small flat paintbrush to paint tread and back of wheel light green. Use damp sponge strip to stamp ¼"w green stripes ¼" apart on tread of wheel. Use small flat paintbrush to paint front of wheel and large end of 1 axle peg red. Use liner paintbrush to paint rim of wheel white. Use pen to draw seeds on front of wheel. Insert axle peg through front of wheel; glue end of peg to bottom of wagon.
7. Knot each end of cord. Glue 1 knot to center bottom of 1 end of wagon.
8. For watermelons, paint eggs light green. Use sponge strip to stamp ¼"w green stripes on eggs.
9. Fill wagon with excelsior. Arrange watermelons in wagon. Glue watermelons together; glue watermelons to excelsior.

WATERMELON WAGON

(Shown on page 27)

You will need an unfinished wooden wagon (we used a 14"w x 19"l x 6"h wagon); white, red, light green, dark green, brown, and black acrylic paint; foam brushes; small round and liner paintbrushes; and one ¾" x 1" piece of cellulose sponge.

1. Remove wheels from wagon.
2. (**Note:** Refer to photo for remaining steps.) Use liner paintbrush and brown paint to paint lines on sides of wagon to make "slats"; while paint is still wet, use a clean paintbrush to apply water to painted lines to soften lines. Use liner paintbrush and brown paint to paint dots to resemble nails at ends of "slats." Allow to dry.
3. (**Note:** Allow to dry after each paint color.) For each wheel, use foam brush to paint tread light green. Use damp sponge piece to stamp ¾"w dark green stripes 1" apart on tread. Use foam brush to paint front of wheel red. Use small round paintbrush to paint black seeds on front of wheel. Use liner paintbrush to paint white highlights on seeds and to paint ⅟₁₆" along edge of front of wheel white.
4. Replace wheels on wagon.

WIRED RIBBON BOWS   (Shown on page 28)

For each bow, you will need one 3" x 44" strip of fabric, two 44" lengths of ⅜"w paper-backed fusible web, 26-gauge paddle wire, wire cutters, liquid fray preventative, hot glue gun, and glue sticks.

1. For wired ribbon, follow manufacturer's instructions to fuse 1 length of web along 1 long edge on wrong side of fabric strip. Remove paper backing.
2. Cut one 46" length of wire; straighten wire length. Center wire length next to web on wrong side of fabric strip; bend each end of wire away from center of fabric strip (**Fig. 1**).

Fig. 1

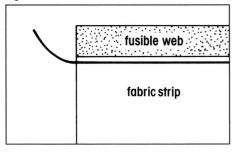

fusible web

fabric strip

3. Working from 1 end of fabric strip to the other, fold webbed edge of fabric ⅜" to wrong side over wire and use tip of iron to lightly "tack" edge of fabric in place. Using tip of iron to push wire into fold of fabric, fuse edge of fabric in place. Trim excess wire.
4. Repeat Steps 1 - 3 for remaining long edge of fabric strip.
5. For bow, cut a 5" length and a 39" length from wired ribbon.
6. Form a 4½" long loop approx. 10½" from 1 end of 39" length of ribbon; gather length between fingers (**Fig. 2a**). Form a second loop same size as first loop; then gather and hold (**Fig. 2b**). Wrap wire tightly around center of bow; trim wire ends close to bow.

Fig. 2a

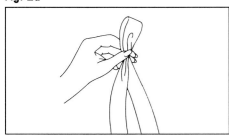

Fig. 2b

7. For bow center, loosely gather 5" length of ribbon lengthwise to form a 1"w gathered length. With wrong side of length facing bow, wrap length around center of bow, overlapping ends at back and trimming excess; glue to secure.
8. Trim bow streamers. Apply fray preventative to ends. Allow to dry.
9. For hanger, thread a 12" length of wire through center back of bow.

PAPIER MÂCHÉ MELONS
(Shown on page 27)

For each melon, you will need 1 small round or oblong balloon, newspaper, liquid starch, light green and dark green acrylic paint, foam brush, one 1" x 2" piece of cellulose sponge, and waxed paper.

1. Cover work surface with waxed paper. Tear or cut newspaper into 1" x 2" and 1" x 5" strips.
2. (**Note:** If a very long balloon is used, knot end of balloon to shorten it before blowing it up to form melon shape.) Blow up balloon and knot opening.
3. Pour starch into a small bowl. Being careful not to saturate strip, use fingers to spread starch on both sides of one 2" newspaper strip. Apply strip to end of balloon close to knot. Overlapping edges of strips and smoothing wrinkles, repeat to apply more 2" strips to end(s) of balloon around knot(s), leaving knot(s) exposed. Repeat to apply 5" strips around remainder of balloon until balloon is covered.
4. Repeat Step 3 to apply 2 more layers of strips to balloon.
5. With 5" strips running lengthwise on balloon, repeat Step 3 again. Hang balloon and allow to dry overnight or until hard and dry.
6. Use a pin to pop balloon. Cut off knot(s).
7. If desired, repeat Step 3 to cover knot hole(s) with small strips of papier mâché; allow to dry.
8. Use foam brush to paint balloon light green; allow to dry. Use damp sponge piece to stamp 1"w to 2"w dark green stripes on balloon. Allow to dry.

WATERMELON TREE SKIRT
(Shown on page 28)

You will need a 50" square of artist's canvas preprimed on 1 side; ¾ yd of 44"w black and white ticking fabric for trim; thread to match fabric; white, red, light green, green, and black acrylic paint; large flat and small round paintbrushes; string or heavy thread; thumbtack or pin; tracing paper; and fabric glue.

1. To mark outer cutting line on primed side (right side) of canvas, tie 1 end of string to a pencil. Insert thumbtack through string 24" from pencil. Insert thumbtack in center of canvas. Mark circle on canvas.
2. To mark inner cutting line, repeat Step 1, inserting thumbtack through string 2" from pencil.
3. Cut out skirt along marked lines. For opening in back of skirt, cut from outer to inner edge.
4. (**Note:** Refer to photo for remaining steps.) On primed side of canvas, use flat paintbrush to paint a 5"w green band along outer curved edge of skirt for rind. While paint is still wet, use a clean flat paintbrush to paint remainder of skirt red, blending red into 1½" of green where the 2 colors meet. Paint light green highlights along inner edge of green part of rind. Allow to dry.
5. For seeds, trace pattern onto tracing paper; cut out. Use a pencil to lightly draw around seed pattern as desired on skirt.
6. Use round paintbrush to paint seeds black; allow to dry. Paint white highlights on seeds; allow to dry.
7. For trim, cut a 2⅜" x 4¼ yd bias strip of fabric, piecing as necessary. Press each long edge of strip ½" to wrong side. Press 1 end of strip ½" to wrong side. Beginning with pressed end at 1 back opening edge of skirt, glue strip along outer curved edge of skirt to within 1" of remaining back opening edge. Trim remaining end of strip to ½" beyond opening edge; press end ½" to wrong side and glue in place.

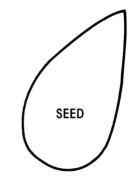

SEED

WATERMELON VINE GARLAND (Shown on page 28)

For each approx. 8-foot-long garland, you will need 7 yds of natural Paper Capers™ Paper Wire; ½ yd of 52"w unprimed artist's canvas; gesso; red, light green, green, and dark green acrylic paint; small flat, large flat, and liner paintbrushes; sunflower seeds; black spray paint; 24-gauge green florist wire; six ¾" dia. red wooden beads; craft knife; tracing paper; wire cutters; hot glue gun; and glue sticks.

1. Trace side piece and bottom piece patterns, this page, onto tracing paper; cut out.
2. (**Note:** Follow Steps 2 - 7 to make 5 watermelon slices.) Matching arrows on patterns to grain of canvas, place patterns on canvas. Use a pencil to draw around patterns on canvas for indicated numbers of pieces; cut out pieces.
3. (**Note:** Refer to photo for remaining steps.) Apply a line of glue along 1 edge of bottom piece. Matching 1 curved edge of 1 side piece to glued edge, press pieces together along edges only. Repeat to glue remaining side piece to remaining edge of bottom piece. Glue remaining (top) edges of side pieces together.
4. Apply 1 coat of gesso to slice; allow to dry.
5. For rind, use large flat paintbrush to paint bottom and ⅝" of sides of slice green. While paint is still wet, use a clean,

large flat paintbrush to paint remainder of sides of slice red, blending red into ¼" of green where the 2 colors meet. Use liner paintbrush to paint light green highlights along top of green part of rind. Use small flat paintbrush to paint ¼"w light green stripes along length of bottom of slice. Allow to dry.
6. For seeds, spray paint sunflower seeds black; allow to dry. Glue seeds to each side of slice.
7. At each end of slice, use craft knife to cut a small "X" for threading slice onto paper wire.
8. Trace leaf patterns, page 33, onto tracing paper; cut out.
9. (**Note:** Follow Steps 9 - 12 to make a total of 7 leaves.) Matching arrow on pattern to grain of canvas, place desired leaf pattern on canvas. Use a pencil to draw around pattern; cut out leaf.
10. Referring to **Fig. 1**, glue a 5½" length of florist wire to small leaf or a 7½" length of florist wire to large leaf.

Fig. 1

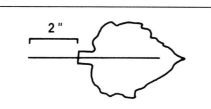

11. Apply gesso to both sides of leaf; allow leaf to curl as it dries.
12. Use large flat paintbrush to paint leaf green. While paint is still wet, use liner paintbrush to paint dark green veins on leaf. Use small flat paintbrush to apply dark green shading to leaf. Use a clean, small flat paintbrush to apply light green highlights to leaf. Allow to dry.
13. For tendrils, cut nine 11" lengths from paper wire. Wrap each wire length tightly around a pencil; remove from pencil and pull ends to separate curls.
14. (**Note:** Follow Steps 14 - 16 to assemble garland.) Tie a loose overhand knot approx. 6" from 1 end of remaining paper wire. Thread 1 bead onto remaining end of paper wire and position bead next to knot. Tie another loose overhand knot next to bead. Thread 1 watermelon slice onto paper wire and position slice approx. 6" from last knot; glue slice to paper wire at each cut "X" to secure. Tying next knot approx. 6" from watermelon slice, repeat to attach remaining beads and slices to garland.
15. To attach each leaf to garland, wrap stem of leaf around paper wire, securing stem by wrapping excess wire tightly around stem.
16. To attach each tendril to garland, tightly wrap 1" at 1 end of tendril around paper wire.
17. Use pencil to curl each end of garland.

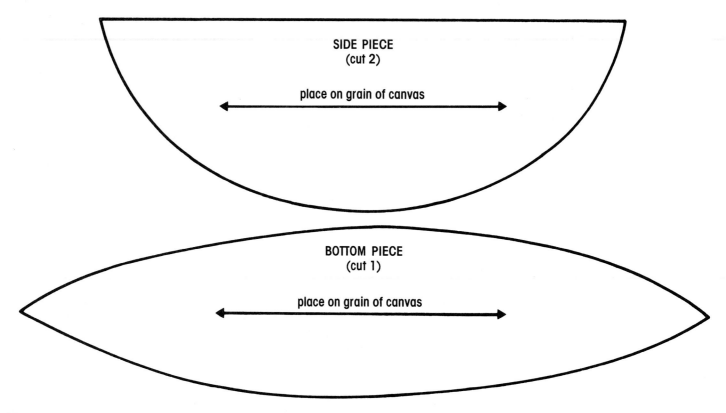

SIDE PIECE
(cut 2)

place on grain of canvas

BOTTOM PIECE
(cut 1)

place on grain of canvas

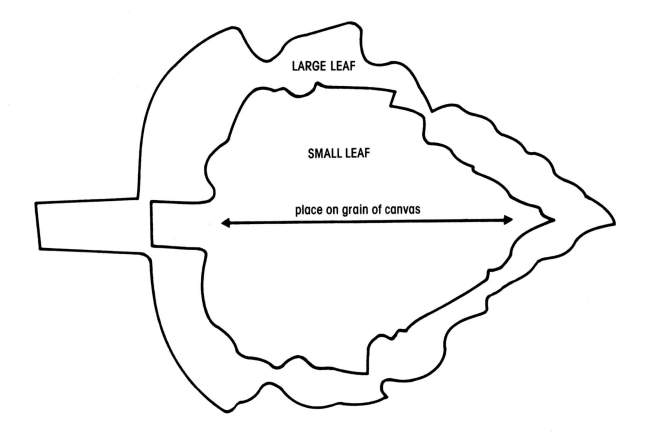

LARGE LEAF

SMALL LEAF

place on grain of canvas

PLACE MATS AND NAPKINS   (Shown on page 29)

For each place mat and napkin, you will need two 13" x 19" pieces of fabric for place mat; one 8" square of artist's canvas preprimed on 1 side for watermelon slice; one 18" square of fabric for napkin; ½"w double-fold bias tape for binding; thread to match napkin fabric and bias tape; paper-backed fusible web; tracing paper; red, green, and light green acrylic paint; small flat and liner paintbrushes; 3 sunflower seeds; black spray paint; removable fabric marking pen; two ¾" dia. VELCRO® brand hook and loop fasteners; VELCRO® brand adhesive; hot glue gun; and glue sticks.

1. For watermelon slice for napkin holder, trace side piece pattern, page 32, onto tracing paper; cut out.
2. Matching arrow on pattern to grain of canvas, place pattern on canvas. Use a pencil to draw around pattern; cut out slice.
3. (**Note:** Refer to photo for remaining steps.) On primed side of slice (front), use small flat paintbrush to paint ⅝" along bottom of slice green for rind. While paint is still wet, use a clean, small flat paintbrush to paint remainder of front of slice red, blending red into ¼" of green where the 2 colors meet. Use liner paintbrush to paint light green highlights along top of green part of rind. Allow to dry.
4. For seeds, spray paint sunflower seeds black; allow to dry. Hot glue seeds to slice.
5. To round off corners of place mat fabric pieces, fold one 13" x 19" fabric piece in half from top to bottom and again from left to right. Place a saucer or can on corner; use fabric marking pen to draw around curve. Cutting through all layers, trim corner along drawn line. Matching wrong sides, place fabric pieces together; use trimmed fabric piece as a pattern to trim corners of remaining fabric piece.
6. For place mat, use 1 fabric piece as a pattern to cut a piece of web. Follow manufacturer's instructions to fuse web to wrong side of fabric piece. Fuse fabric pieces wrong sides together.

7. For binding, measure around place mat; add 1". Cut a length of bias tape the determined measurement.
8. Unfold 1 end of binding and press ½" to wrong side; refold binding. Beginning with unpressed end of binding, insert raw edge of place mat into fold of binding. Stitching close to inner edge of binding, sew binding in place.
9. To attach watermelon slice to place mat, use VELCRO® adhesive to glue hook side of 1 fastener to each corner on wrong side of slice. Place slice on place mat with middle of slice raised to allow room for napkin; use fabric marking pen to mark placement for loop side of each fastener on place mat. Glue loop sides of fasteners to place mat at marks. Attach slice to place mat.
10. For napkin, machine stitch ½" from edges of fabric square; fringe fabric to stitching line.
11. Remove slice before laundering place mat.

A FESTIVAL OF TREES

Decorating the Christmas tree is one of the season's best-loved activities. With eager anticipation, we unpack our boxes of treasured ornaments and trimmings. What fun we have dressing the fragrant branches in Yuletide finery! In addition to the traditional tree in the living room, smaller trees are a wonderful — and unexpected — way to bring Christmas spirit to other areas of the house as well. Choose your favorite (or favorites!) from the collection of five decorating themes offered here to add an extra special touch to your holiday celebration. Instructions for the projects begin on page 42.

Rich tones of red, gold, and green give the stately **Poinsettia Tree** (*page 44*) an air of elegance. Holly and poinsettia ornaments are fashioned from velvet ribbon and feature shiny berries in contrasting colors. Gold mesh ribbon and a red and gold bead garland add to the traditional look. With its handsome plaid ruffle, the red velvet tree skirt harmonizes with the other decorations. *Opposite*: The beautiful trimmings from the tree also adorn a purchased wreath to create a lovely coordinating accent.

(*Opposite*) The ''**Save the Earth**'' **Tree** (*page 46*) is an imaginative way to express your concern for our planet and its endangered species. A stenciled cedar tree topper conveys your thoughtful message, and painted earth ornaments represent the planet entrusted to our care. Stenciled fabric ornaments portray endangered animals that need our protection. A river of blue twisted paper winds among the tree branches, and pinecones and holly add a natural touch. To show your commitment to preserving our planet's natural resources, leave the tree's root ball intact so the tree can be replanted after the festivities are over. This year, show your true Christmas color: green!

Sailors and landlubbers alike will be delighted by this **Nautical Tree** (*page 42*). Lobster and fish ornaments share the branches with miniature life preservers and icicles fashioned from corks. ''Bobbers'' are easy to create by dipping red glass ball ornaments into white paint. To add holiday spirit, a plastic canvas signal flag garland spells ''Merry Christmas.'' Fun finishing touches include a lighthouse tree topper and a fishnet tree skirt. Ornaments from the tree can also double as cute package decorations.

(*Opposite*) The downhill skiers on this adorable **Penguin Tree** (*page 45*) are having plenty of frosty fun! Wearing little red flannel mittens and a hat, each cheerful bird has its own pair of skis and poles. The sparkling ornaments include resin ice cubes, snow-capped silver glass balls, and plastic icicles. Drifts of cotton batting "snow" and a snowflake garland and tree topper round out the decorations. A fringed muffler continues the wintry theme at the bottom of the tree, where a trio of penguins skis beside an icy lake.

Playfully prancing around the **Kitty-Cat Tree** (*page 45*), these cardboard kitties feature button joints and movable legs. The fanciful felines are unraveling balls of yarn as they frolic among "catnip" baskets filled with dried sweet Annie. Other decorations include a wooden bead garland and bows fashioned from torn fabric strips. Topping the tree in "purr-fect" style is the Kitty-Cat Motel — a re-decorated birdhouse! A length of calico fabric wraps the base of the tree in cozy country style.

NAUTICAL TREE (Shown on page 39)

Whether your domain is on land or sea, this bright four-foot-tall tree will welcome friends aboard for a happy holiday. Keeping watch over the tree is the Lighthouse Tree Topper. Cork ''Icicles,'' along with Life Preserver Ornaments, Lobster Ornaments, and Fish Ornaments, contribute to the maritime atmosphere. ''Bobber'' ornaments are crafted by dipping purchased red glass ball ornaments into white enamel paint and hanging them to dry. Fishing nets skirt the base of the tree, and from every bough, the plastic canvas Flag Garland signals to one and all — ''MERRY CHRISTMAS!''

LIGHTHOUSE TREE TOPPER

You will need three white 16 oz. plastic foam cups; one 5" square of ¼" thick foam core board; one 5" square of heavy paper; yellow, red, blue, grey, and black acrylic paint; small round paintbrushes; craft glue; craft knife; cutting mat or thick layer of newspapers; black permanent felt-tip pen with fine point; tracing paper; and compass.

1. Trace door and window patterns onto tracing paper; cut out.
2. (**Note:** Refer to photo for remaining steps.) Turn cups upside down. Use a pencil to draw around door pattern on rim of 1 cup. Set second cup aside. Spacing windows evenly, draw around arch window pattern on rim and round window pattern on side of third cup.
3. (**Note:** Allow to dry after each paint color or glue step.) On first cup, paint door red and remainder of rim grey. Paint rim of second cup red. On third cup, paint windows yellow; leaving ⅛" of white at bottom of rim, paint remainder of rim blue.
4. Referring to patterns, use black paint to paint outlines and detail lines on door and windows. Use black paint to paint outlines of stones in grey area of first cup.
5. Use compass to draw a 3¼" dia. circle on foam board. Use craft knife to cut out circle. Paint circle black.
6. For tower, cut a 1½" x 5" strip from heavy paper. Paint a ¾"w yellow stripe ¼" from 1 long edge (top) of strip. Paint remainder of strip black. Use pen to draw lines ¼" apart along length and across width of yellow stripe to make a grid. Overlap ends of strip ¼" and glue together to form a cylinder.
7. For tower roof, use compass to draw a 3" dia. circle on heavy paper; cut out circle. Cut out one quarter of circle and discard. Paint paper shape black. Overlapping straight edges approx. ¼", glue edges together to form a cone.
8. To assemble lighthouse, glue cups together. Glue foam board circle on cups, tower on circle, and roof on tower.

FISH ORNAMENTS

For each ornament, you will need a 3½" x 7½" piece of 1/16" thick cork, black permanent felt-tip pen with fine point, blue and yellow acrylic paint, paintbrushes, 8" of nylon line (for hanger), tracing paper, graphite transfer paper, utility scissors, hot glue gun, and glue sticks.

1. Trace desired fish pattern onto tracing paper.
2. Using transfer paper and a dull pencil, transfer pattern onto cork.
3. (**Note:** Refer to photo for remaining steps.) Use pen to draw over transferred lines and to draw remaining detail lines and scales.
4. Dilute blue paint with water. Brush diluted paint on fish as desired; allow to dry. Using undiluted blue and yellow paint, paint details on fish; allow to dry.
5. Cut out fish.
6. Knot ends of nylon line together; glue knot to top center back of fish.

LIFE PRESERVER ORNAMENTS

For each ornament, you will need two 8" squares of white fabric, white thread, polyester fiberfill, four 6" lengths of ¼"w blue grosgrain ribbon, 25" of ⅛" dia. white cotton cord, tracing paper, fabric marking pencil, compass, hot glue gun, and glue sticks.

1. For pattern, use compass to draw a 6½" dia. circle on tracing paper; draw a 2½" dia. circle in center of first circle. Cut along drawn lines.
2. Center pattern on wrong side of 1 fabric square; use fabric marking pencil to draw around pattern. Do not cut out shape.
3. Place fabric squares right sides together. Sew squares together directly on pencil lines.
4. Leaving a ¼" seam allowance, cut out shape; clip seam allowances. For opening for turning, cut through shape from outer to inner edge. Turn shape right side out.
5. Stuff shape firmly with fiberfill. Fold raw edges ¼" to wrong side; whipstitch ends together.
6. (**Note:** Refer to photo for remaining steps.) Forming a ⅝" loop at outside seam and overlapping ribbon ends ¼" at inside seam, glue 1 ribbon length around stuffed shape, covering hand-stitched seam. Spacing ribbon lengths evenly, repeat to glue remaining lengths around stuffed shape.
7. Loosely thread cord through ribbon loops. Knot each end of cord. Knot ends of cord together.

CORK ''ICICLES''

For each ''icicle,'' you will need 4 corks in graduated sizes (we used ⅝"h to 1¼"h corks), hammer, nail, 10" of jute twine, large needle, Design Master® glossy wood tone spray (available at craft stores and florist shops), hot glue gun, and glue sticks.

1. (**Note:** Refer to photo for all steps.) Using hammer and nail, carefully punch a hole through center of each cork.
2. Thread needle with twine; knot 1 end. Leaving ½" of twine between corks, thread corks onto twine from smallest to largest.
3. For hanger, glue remaining end of twine to center top of large cork, forming a loop.
4. Lightly spray ''icicle'' with wood tone spray. Allow to dry.

LOBSTER ORNAMENTS

For each ornament, you will need 1 approx. 8" x 10" plastic foam meat tray (available in meat department of grocery store), red and black acrylic paint, foam brushes, glossy clear acrylic spray, two 4mm black beads, 16" of 18-gauge florist wire, tracing paper, craft knife, cutting mat or thick layer of newspapers, wire cutters, craft glue, hot glue gun, and glue sticks.

1. Use lobster pattern and follow **Tracing Patterns,** page 158.
2. Place pattern in meat tray with tail on upturned tray edge. Use a dull pencil to draw around pattern on tray; draw over detail lines of pattern to lightly indent lines into tray. Remove pattern. Use pencil to press detail lines deeper into tray. Use craft knife to cut out lobster.

3. Allowing to dry between coats, apply 2 coats of red paint and 1 coat of acrylic spray to lobster.

4. For eyes, refer to photo and use craft glue to glue beads to lobster; allow to dry.

5. For antennas, cut wire in half. Paint wires black; allow to dry. Bend a curve into 1 end of each wire. Refer to photo and hot glue 1" at straight end of each wire to back of lobster.

FLAG GARLAND

For each garland, you will need fourteen 2" x 2½" pieces (14 x 18 threads) of 7 mesh plastic canvas, #16 tapestry needle, worsted weight yarn (see color key), and ¼" dia. white cotton cord.

1. Follow charts and use Tent Stitch, Backstitch, and Overcast Stitch, page 159, to work flags to spell "MERRY CHRISTMAS."

2. For each flag, refer to photo and use matching yarn to form two ⅜" loops on top back corners.

3. Thread cord through loops on flags, spacing flags as desired. Knot each end of cord.

"MERRY CHRISTMAS" FLAGS
(14 x 18 threads each)

white
yellow
red
blue
black

M

E

R

Y

C

H

I

S

T

A

POINSETTIA TREE (Shown on page 37)

An elegant holiday is assured for the home graced by this classic seven-foot-tall tree. Gold mesh ribbon fashioned into bows, loops, and streamers and red and gold bead garland provide a rich setting for the handmade Poinsettias and Holly Sprigs. A red velvet Tree Skirt trimmed with gold lamé cording and a plaid ruffle encircles the base of the tree.

TREE SKIRT

You will need one 36" square of red velvet fabric for tree skirt top, one 36" square of fabric for tree skirt lining, one 14"w bias strip of plaid fabric 9 yds long for ruffle (pieced as necessary), 3 yds of purchased ¾" dia. gold lamé cording, thread to match fabrics, string, fabric marking pencil, and thumbtack or pin.

1. Fold lining fabric in half from top to bottom and again from left to right.
2. To mark outer cutting line, tie 1 end of string to fabric marking pencil. Insert thumbtack through string 16½" from pencil. Insert thumbtack in fabric as shown in **Fig. 1** and mark ¼ of a circle.

Fig. 1

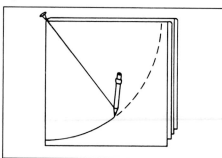

3. To mark inner cutting line, repeat Step 2, inserting thumbtack through string 2" from pencil.
4. Cutting through all layers of fabric, cut out lining along marked lines. For opening in back of lining, cut through 1 thickness of fabric along 1 fold from outer to inner edge.
5. Place lining and skirt top fabric right sides together. Use lining as a pattern to cut skirt top from fabric.
6. Matching raw edges, baste cording along outer edge on right side of skirt top, trimming cording to fit. At each end of cording, open fabric and trim 1" from cotton cord.

7. For ruffle, fold fabric strip in half lengthwise with wrong sides together; do not press. To gather ruffle, place string ⅜" from long raw edge of ruffle. Use a wide zigzag stitch to stitch over string, being careful not to catch string in stitching. Pull string, gathering ruffle to fit outer edge of skirt top.
8. Matching right sides and raw edges, baste ruffle to outer edge of skirt top over cording.
9. Place skirt top and lining right sides together. Use a ½" seam allowance to sew inner curved edges together. Using a zipper foot and stitching as close as possible to cording, sew outer curved edges together. Clip seam allowances and turn right side out. Leaving ruffle unpressed, press skirt.
10. Press each straight edge of skirt, including ruffle, ½" toward lining; press ½" toward lining again and stitch in place.

POINSETTIAS AND HOLLY SPRIGS

For each poinsettia, you will need 2½"w red single-faced velvet ribbon (2½ yds for large poinsettia, 2 yds for small poinsettia), Design Master® cranberry spray paint (available at craft stores or florist shops), and 1 gold berry cluster (1½" dia. for large poinsettia, 1" dia. for small poinsettia).
For each holly sprig, you will need ¾ yd of 2"w green single-faced velvet ribbon and one 1" dia. red berry cluster.
You will also need a dull knife or stylus, 24-gauge florist wire, green florist tape, permanent felt-tip pen with fine point, newspapers, tracing paper, wire cutters, hot glue gun, and glue sticks.

POINSETTIA

1. Lightly spray right side of ribbon unevenly with cranberry paint; allow to dry.
2. Trace inner, middle, and outer petal patterns for desired size poinsettia onto tracing paper; cut out.
3. Use pen to draw around each pattern 5 times on wrong side of ribbon; cut out petals.
4. For veins on each petal, place petal right side up on a thick layer of newspapers. Referring to photo, page 36, use knife to score veins on petal, being careful not to cut through ribbon.
5. Cut a length of wire same length as each petal. Center and glue wire lengthwise on wrong side of petal.
6. For flower stem, cut a 1½" length of wire. Use florist tape to tape berry cluster to 1 end of wire.
7. With right sides of petals facing berry cluster, position inner petals 1 at a time around berry cluster, wrapping stems with florist tape. Repeat using middle petals, then outer petals. Arrange petals as desired.

HOLLY SPRIG

1. Trace holly leaf pattern onto tracing paper; cut out.
2. To make holly leaves and stem, follow Steps 3 - 6 of Poinsettia instructions.
3. With right sides of leaves facing berry cluster, position leaves 1 at a time around berry cluster, wrapping stems with florist tape. Arrange leaves as desired.

SMALL MIDDLE PETAL

LARGE MIDDLE PETAL

SMALL/LARGE INNER PETAL

SMALL OUTER PETAL

LARGE OUTER PETAL

PENGUIN TREE (Shown on page 40)

From the giant snowflake at its top to the woolly scarf around its base, this four-foot-tall tree brings to mind the joys of winter. Artificial snow, icicles, snowflake garland, and snowdrifts made from cotton batting set the scene for some slippery fun. The Penguin Ornaments, made from plastic foam eggs covered with papier mâché, ski about the snow-covered scene. A mirror, its edges covered with cotton batting and artificial snow, becomes a penguin-sized pond. The tops of the silver glass ball ornaments were sprayed with spray adhesive and sprinkled with artificial snow for a frosty look. For the ice cube ornaments, we filled a plastic ice cube tray with Castin' Craft casting resin; for each hanger, we knotted the ends of a 6" length of nylon line together and placed the knot in one corner of each cube before the resin hardened.

PENGUIN ORNAMENTS

For each ornament, you will need a 3"h plastic foam egg; instant papier mâché (we used Celluclay® Instant Papier Mâché); white, orange, and black acrylic paint; paintbrushes; two 2" x 4" pieces of red flannel for mittens; one 6½" x 10" piece of red flannel for hat; paper-backed fusible web; one ½" white pom-pom; two 16mm black spoke sequins; 2 jumbo wooden craft sticks; 2 bamboo skewers; utility scissors; Design Master® glossy wood tone spray (available at craft stores and florist shops); red thread; tracing paper; hot glue gun; and glue sticks.

1. Follow **Papier Mâché** instructions, page 158, to apply a smooth ⅛" thick layer of papier mâché to egg.
2. (**Note:** Refer to photo for remaining steps. Allow to dry after each paint color.) Paint egg black. For shirt, paint a 1¼" x 1⅝" white oval on egg; paint black buttons on shirt. For face, paint white eyes and an orange beak.
3. Use hat and mitten patterns and follow **Tracing Patterns**, page 158.
4. For hat, use pattern to cut hat from flannel piece. Matching right sides and curved edges, fold hat piece in half. Using a ¼" seam allowance, sew curved edges together. Hand baste ¼" from small end (top) of hat. Pull basting thread, tightly gathering top of hat; knot and trim thread. Turn hat right side out.
5. For hat cuff, press bottom edge of hat 1½" to wrong side; press bottom edge ¾" to right side. Glue hat to penguin; push top of hat down. Glue pom-pom to hat.
6. For skis, trim 1 end of each craft stick to a point. Spray craft sticks lightly with wood tone spray.
7. For each ski pole, cut a 4" length from pointed end of 1 skewer; discard remainder. Paint ¾" at cut end of skewer black. Slide sequin onto pointed end of skewer; glue to secure.
8. For mittens, follow manufacturer's instructions and use web to fuse flannel pieces wrong sides together. Use pattern to cut 2 mittens from fused flannel.
9. Glue mittens, ski poles, and skis to penguin.

HAT

KITTY-CAT TREE (Shown on page 41)

Cat-lover or not, who could resist this cute tree? Not our feline friend who lounges on the calico fabric we used for a tree skirt! Our frisky Kitty-Cat Ornaments play among the wooden bead garland and fabric bows on this four-foot-tall tree. Yarn balls and small baskets of "CATNIP" (we used dried sweet Annie) provide a little rest and recreation. For the Kitty-Cat Motel atop our tree, we painted a wooden birdhouse ornament cream with a red roof and dark grey base. We used sponge pieces cut into stone shapes to sponge paint grey and dark grey stones on the birdhouse. A black paint pen was used to write "Kitty-Cat Motel." The "VACANCY" sign is simply a piece of white paper glued to a craft stick. The entire tree topper was sprayed lightly with Design Master® glossy wood tone spray (available at craft stores or florist shops).

KITTY-CAT ORNAMENTS

For each ornament, you will need corrugated cardboard, acrylic paint (see Steps 2, 4, and 5 for colors), foam brush, small round paintbrushes, black permanent felt-tip pen with fine point, 4 buttons, ecru embroidery floss, large sharp needle, compass, cellulose sponge, tracing paper, craft knife, and cutting mat or thick layer of newspapers.

1. Trace body and leg patterns onto tracing paper; cut out. Draw around body pattern once and each leg pattern twice on cardboard; use craft knife to cut out pieces.
2. (**Note:** Refer to photo for remaining steps. Allow to dry after each paint step.) Painting both sides of cardboard pieces, use foam brush to paint tabby cat with grey paint, dark grey cat with dark grey paint, or calico cat with cream paint.
3. For tabby cat, trace stripe pattern onto tracing paper and cut out; use pattern to cut 3 stripe pieces from sponge. For dark grey cat, cut one 1" dia. circle from sponge. For calico cat, cut three 1" dia. circles from sponge.
4. (**Note:** Before sponge painting, dampen sponge pieces.) For tabby cat, use 1 stripe sponge for each color of paint and stamp dark grey, light grey, and white stripes on cat pieces. For dark grey cat, use circle sponge to stamp face, ear, paws, and tip of tail with cream paint. For calico cat, use 1 circle sponge for each color of paint and stamp brown, rust, and dark yellow spots on cat pieces.
5. Use small round paintbrush to paint black eyes and pink nose on cat. Use pen to draw whiskers.

6. (**Note:** Refer to patterns to assemble ornament.) To attach front legs to body, thread needle with floss; knot ends together. Bring needle up through 1 leg at ●, through body at ●, and through remaining leg at ●. Pull floss until legs are tight against body. Thread needle through 1 button and take needle back down through legs and body. Thread needle through a second button and bring needle back up through legs and body. Repeat to make several more stitches through buttons, legs, and body. Knot floss at back of ornament; trim ends. Repeat to attach back legs to body at ■.

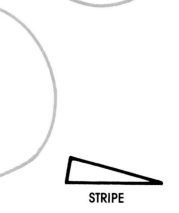

STRIPE

"SAVE THE EARTH" TREE (Shown on page 38)

With its Earth Ornaments and Endangered Species Ornaments, this live evergreen tree conveys a concern for our planet and the many animals who share it with us. A garland of brilliant blue Paper Capers® twisted paper, untwisted and sprayed lightly with Design Master® glossy wood tone spray (available at craft stores and florist shops), represents the waters of the earth. Preserved holly and springerii fern, natural and bleached pinecones, and longleaf pine picks are tucked among the ornaments and garland. A sign at the top of the tree urges us to "SAVE THE EARTH." A purchased lettering stencil was used to paint the message on a piece of cedar board, and twigs were hot glued around its edges. The root ball of the tree is wrapped in brown craft paper.

EARTH ORNAMENTS

For each ornament, you will need one 3" dia. clear plastic ball container ornament (available at craft stores); tracing paper; Miracle Sponges™ (dry, compressed sponges available at craft stores); plastic or coated paper plates; white, blue, light green, and green acrylic paint; and permanent felt-tip pen with fine point.

1. Trace continent patterns, this page, onto tracing paper; cut out.
2. Use pen to draw around continent patterns on dry sponge; cut out sponge shapes. Cut 2 small pieces from remaining sponge.
3. Separate ornament into halves.
4. (**Note:** Refer to photo for remaining steps.) Dampen sponge pieces. Swirl small amounts of white and blue paint together on a plate to achieve a marbled effect. Using 1 small sponge piece, lightly stamp insides of ornament halves with swirled paint mixture. Allow to dry.
5. With hanging tab of each ornament half at top, use continent sponge shapes and green paint to stamp continents on outsides of ornament halves.
6. Using remaining small sponge piece and light green paint, stamp highlights on continents. Allow to dry.
7. Reassemble ornament.

ENDANGERED SPECIES ORNAMENTS

For each ornament, you will need one 8" square of brown fabric, one 8" square of poster board, acetate for stencils (available at craft stores), permanent felt-tip pen with fine point, craft knife, cutting mat or thick layer of newspapers, acrylic paint (see color key), stencil brushes, small round paintbrush, liner paintbrushes, removable tape (optional), paper towels, ¼"w jute braid trim (for trim and hanger), spray adhesive, and craft glue.

1. Referring to stencil cutting key and color key, follow **Stenciling**, page 158, to stencil desired animal design, this page or page 47, at center of fabric square. Referring to photo and color key, use small round and liner paintbrushes to paint remaining details. Allow to dry.
2. Use spray adhesive to glue poster board to wrong side of stenciled fabric.
3. Referring to photo, cut out ornament ½" outside stenciled design.

4. Beginning at bottom of ornament, use craft glue to glue jute braid trim around edge of ornament, trimming to fit.
5. For hanger, cut a 6" length of trim; fold in half to form a loop. Use craft glue to glue ends to top center back of ornament.

STENCIL CUTTING KEY

- ▦ Stencil #1
- ▦ Stencil #2
- ▦ Stencil #3

COLOR KEY
WHALE
- Stencil #1 — ivory
- Stencil #2 — very dark grey
- Eye — ivory
- Highlight in eye — white

ELEPHANT
- Stencil #1 — dark grey highlighted with grey
- Stencil #2 (ear and toenails) — grey
- Stencil #2 (tusk) — white
- Eye — black
- Highlight in eye — white

EAGLE
- Stencil #1 — very dark grey
- Stencil #2 — white
- Stencil #3 (wings) — grey
- Stencil #3 (beak and feet) — dark yellow
- Eye and talons — black
- Highlight in eye — white

DOLPHIN
- Stencil #1 — white
- Stencil #2 — dark grey highlighted with grey
- Eye — black
- Highlight in eye — white

OWL
- Stencil #1 — white
- Stencil #2 (wing) — light grey highlighted with white
- Stencil #2 (dark areas around eyes) — light grey
- Stencil #3 — dark yellow
- Pupils of eyes — black
- Highlights in eyes — white

PANDA
- Stencil #1 — white
- Stencil #2 — black
- Eyes — brown
- Highlights in eyes — white

NUTCRACKER PARADE

For more than a hundred Christmases, the nutcracker has been one of our most beloved Yuletide characters. His touching story, fancifully told in the classic holiday ballet, is an enchanting one for children and adults alike, filling us with a sense of wonder and excitement.

Awaiting the magical moment when he, too, may be transformed into the handsome prince of a little girl's dreams, each of these nutcrackers has his own unique personality. The soldiers, attired in splendid uniforms embellished with gold trims and buttons, stand at attention, ready to fall into marching formation at a minute's notice.

To keep the beat for the nutcrackers' dream parade, little toy drums and an array of musical motifs can be found throughout this collection. The plaid tree skirt and a coordinating fringed throw are adorned with appliquéd drums and melodious notes. Rounding out the decorations, a needlepoint nutcracker makes a splendid addition to a pillow.

The spirit of Christmas will march into your home this year with these proud nutcrackers and their musical accessories. Instructions for the projects begin on page 52.

Dressed up with gold trimmings, the needlepoint **Nutcracker Pillow** (*page 56*) makes a rich holiday accent. Handsome and practical, the fringed wool **Appliquéd Throw** (*page 52*) repeats the color scheme and melodic theme from the tree decorations. *Opposite*: A company of **Small**, **Medium**, and **Large Nutcrackers** (*pages 54 and 55*) stands at attention on the **Nutcracker Tree** (*page 52*). Musical motifs, including **Toy Drums** (*page 53*), keep the beat for the nutcrackers' Christmas parade. Miniature candle lights, glass ball ornaments, bows and jingle bells, sprigs of holly, and bead garlands make an attractive backdrop for the soldiers. The lyrical theme continues at the bottom of the tree with the plaid **Appliquéd Tree Skirt** (*page 52*).

NUTCRACKER PILLOW (Shown on page 51)

For an approx. 18"x 12" pillow, you will need one 10" x 16" piece of 14 mesh needlepoint canvas; gold (002) Kreinik Balger® Heavy (#32) Braid and Paternayan Persian yarn (see color key); #22 tapestry needle; masking tape; one 10" x 16" piece of fabric for stitched piece backing; two 13" x 19" pieces of fabric for pillow top and back; two 13½" lengths of ¼" dia. gold cording with ½"w seam allowance; two 13" lengths of ³⁄₁₆"w gold braid trim; two 13" lengths of ½"w gold ribbon; two 13" lengths of 1"w gold loop fringe; thread to match fabrics and trims; polyester fiberfill; and blocking board, spray bottle filled with water, and T-pins (optional).

1. Cover edges of canvas with masking tape.
2. Following chart and using Tent Stitch and Backstitch, page 57, work design on canvas, using 2 strands of yarn or 1 strand of gold braid for Tent Stitch and 1 strand of yarn for Backstitch.
3. (**Note:** Follow Step 3 to block stitched piece or have an experienced dry cleaner clean and block stitched piece.) To block stitched piece, dampen stitched piece with water. Place stitched piece on blocking board and align canvas threads with horizontal and vertical lines on board. Use T-pins, spaced ½" apart, to pin stitched piece to board. Allow to dry; remove pins.

4. Trim canvas ½" from stitched design. Cut backing fabric same size as canvas.
5. Matching raw edge of 1 cording length to 1 long edge of stitched piece, use zipper foot and baste cording to right side of stitched piece; trim cording to fit. Repeat for remaining long edge of stitched piece.
6. For panel, place stitched piece and backing fabric right sides together. Using a zipper foot and stitching as close as possible to cording, sew stitched piece and backing together along long edges. Turn right side out and press.
7. (**Note:** Refer to photo for remaining steps.) For pillow top, center stitched panel between short edges on right side of 1 pillow fabric piece (top). Baste top and bottom edges of panel to fabric piece.

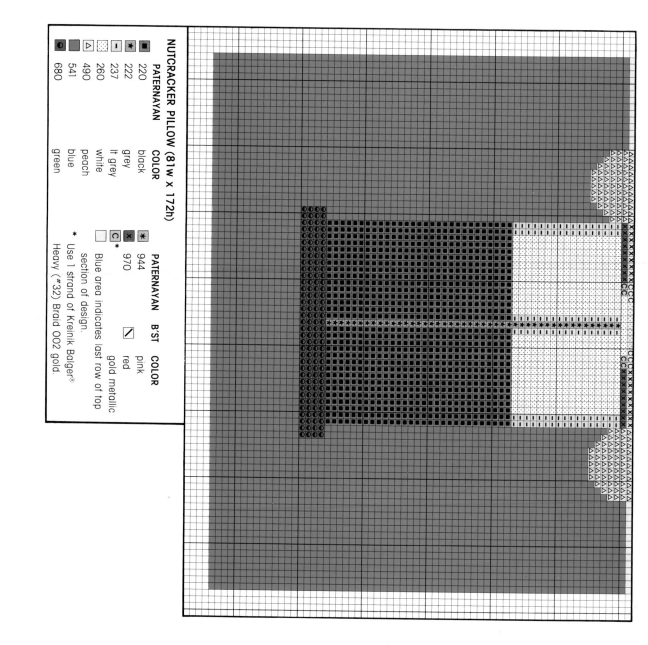

NUTCRACKER PILLOW (81w x 172h)

	PATERNAYAN	COLOR
◑	220	black
▨	222	grey
▷	237	lt grey
⦂	260	white
❘	490	peach
✳	541	blue
▪	680	green

	PATERNAYAN	B'ST	COLOR
☐			
C	944		pink
✕	970		red
✳			gold metallic
		╱	red

* Blue area indicates last row of top section of design.

* Use 1 strand of Kreinik Balger® Heavy (#32) Braid 002 gold.

56

8. For trims along right edge of stitched panel on pillow top, place 1 length of gold braid trim on pillow top 1" from cording on stitched panel; using a medium width zigzag stitch with medium stitch length, stitch over trim. Place 1 length of ribbon on pillow top ½" from gold braid trim. Place straight edge of 1 length of loop fringe ⅛" under right edge of ribbon. Using a straight stitch and stitching along long edges of ribbon, sew ribbon and fringe to pillow top. Repeat for trims along left edge of stitched panel.

9. Place pillow top and back right sides together. Leaving an opening for turning, use a ½" seam allowance to sew top and back together. Cut corners diagonally, turn right side out, and press. Stuff pillow with fiberfill. Sew final closure by hand.

TENT STITCH

Work 1 Tent Stitch to correspond to each square on the chart. When working a single row of Tent Stitches horizontally, vertically, or diagonally, use the Continental method (**Fig. 1a**). When working an area having several rows of stitches, use the Basketweave method (**Fig. 1b**).

Fig. 1a

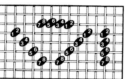

Fig. 1b

BACKSTITCH

This stitch is worked over completed stitches to outline or define (**Fig. 2**). It is sometimes worked over more than 1 thread.

Fig. 2

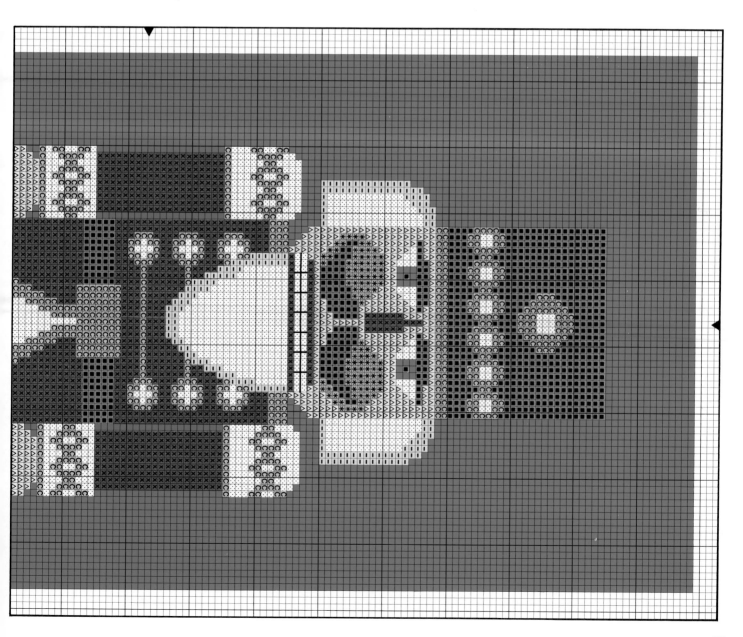

GIFTS OF THE MAGI

*T*he three Wise Men who traveled from afar to honor the newborn King are among the most enthralling players in the Christmas story. Reflecting the regal status of the Magi, this magnificent collection glimmers and gleams with splendid decorations in royal colors. The handcrafted Wise Men are the focal point of the tree as they follow the gold mesh ribbon road to Bethlehem, represented by the Christmas star tree topper. Along their journey are sparkling jewel boxes and crowns, handmade tassels and embellished stars, a dazzling array of purchased ornaments and garlands, and tiny gold lights. At the base, luxurious purple satin and gold mesh fabrics provide a lavish backdrop for packages wrapped in elegant gift paper. Hanging from the mantel, rich stockings provide the crowning touch to this majestic collection. Instructions for the projects begin on page 64.

Bearing gifts worthy of a king, the Magi arrived in Bethlehem to celebrate the birth of Jesus. In addition to lending a stately air to the tree, these splendid **Wise Men** (*page 66*) make a grand arrangement for a table or mantel.

Majestic ornaments in royal colors adorn the magnificent **Gifts of the Magi Tree** (*page 64*). **Crown Ornaments** (*page 68*) and **Jewel Box Ornaments** (*page 65*) are dressed up with lavish fabrics and colorful jewel stones. Gold fabric and bead garland lend richness to the **Tassel Ornaments** (*page 65*). The embellished star ornament on the treetop **Christmas Star** (*page 65*) also appears on the branches of the tree. Tiny lights and medallion ornaments add a golden glow, and shimmering glass ornaments, garlands of beads and stars, and glittery gold spirals complete the elegant trimmings.

The sponge-painted **Jewel Box Card Holder** (*page 64*) is padded with fabric on the inside. Adorned with gold trims and tassels and a medallion ornament on the lid, the lovely box can be used to display Christmas cards during the holidays. Afterwards, it will make an attractive jewelry box.

These **Fancy Gift Wraps** (*page 64*) make any package fit for a king! The wraps are fun to create by painting clear cellophane and foil wrapping paper using sponges and fan brushes. Ornaments from the tree make memorable package decorations.

A striking Christmas decoration for a bare wall can be created by trimming a wall tree with a colorful array of ornaments from the **Gifts of the Magi Tree** (*page 64*).

(*Opposite*) Echoing the **Crown Ornaments** (*page 68*) on the tree, the **Regal Stockings** (*page 68*) are embellished with gold tassels and braid. Little gifts found in these richly colored stockings are sure to make a grand impression on Christmas morning.

GIFTS OF THE MAGI TREE
(Shown on page 59)

Portraying the journey of the Magi, this brilliant tree will add a regal touch to any Christmas decor.

Brightly colored glass ornaments in a variety of shapes and sizes reflect the gleaming lights strung on the tree, while garlands of colorful beads and golden stars twine among the branches. Delicate spirals of gold curly ting-ting purchased at a florist shop sparkle amid the ornaments and garlands.

Other purchased ornaments are transformed to coordinate with the opulent colors of the tree. Resembling ornate frames, medallion tree ornaments are embellished with additional jewel stones, tassels, and shining wire mesh ribbon. The 7" wide filigree star ornaments are given royal treatment when they are dressed up with rich fabrics and jewel stones.

The 12" wide gold mesh ribbon that winds to the top of the tree represents the road to Bethlehem which the Wise Men (page 66) are following. Easily made using simple sculpting and sewing techniques, these richly robed dolls enhance the tree or make a splendid table centerpiece.

Elegantly painted and trimmed Jewel Box Ornaments (page 65) are placed on the tree, ready to hold small gifts for loved ones. Regal Crown Ornaments (page 68) are made by covering and trimming a plastic foam half ball. Crafted from gold bead garland and shiny fabrics and trims, oversized Tassel Ornaments (page 65) add to the grandeur of the scene.

At the top of the tree, the shining Christmas Star (page 65) provides a beacon for the Magi on their journey. The painted cardboard star is trimmed with gold cord, glitter, and one of the embellished star ornaments.

A tree skirt, made by draping purple satin and gold mesh fabrics together, provides the final touch for this majestic Christmas celebration.

JEWEL BOX CARD HOLDER
(Shown on page 61)

You will need an unfinished wooden box with hinged lid (we used a 6"w x 12"l x 6¼"h box), metallic gold spray paint, light purple and dark purple acrylic paint, 2 pieces of natural sponge, paintbrush, gold trims, poster board, metallic gold fabric, polyester bonded batting, 16" gold cord napkin tie with 1½" long tassels, decorative upholstery tack, purchased gold medallion ornament with hanger removed, craft glue, hot glue gun, and glue sticks.

1. Spray paint inside and outside of box gold; allow to dry.
2. Dampen 1 sponge piece. Use sponge piece to lightly stamp inside and outside of box lid and outside of box with dark purple paint. Repeat using light purple paint. Allow to dry.
3. Use paintbrush to paint trim on box, top edges of box, and edges of box lid dark purple. Allow to dry.
4. (**Note:** Use craft glue for gluing unless otherwise indicated.) To line box, measure length and width of 1 side on inside of box. Cut a piece of poster board the determined measurements. Cut a piece of batting same size as poster board. Cut a piece of fabric 1" larger on all sides than batting piece. Glue batting to poster board. Center poster board, batting side down, on wrong side of fabric. Alternating sides and pulling fabric taut, glue edges of fabric to wrong side of poster board. Hot glue wrong side of covered poster board to inside of box. Repeat to line remaining 3 sides and bottom of box.
5. Referring to photo, glue trims around box as desired. Glue straight edge of trim along edge on wrong side of medallion ornament. Hot glue ornament to inside center of box lid. Tie napkin tie into a bow. Use tack to attach bow to center front of box lid.

FANCY GIFT WRAPS
(Shown on page 61)

GOLD FOIL GIFT WRAP
You will need gold foil wrapping paper, blue acrylic paint, and natural sponge piece.

Dampen sponge piece. Using a light stamping motion, use sponge to randomly stamp wrapping paper with paint. Allow to dry.

PURPLE FOIL GIFT WRAP
You will need purple foil wrapping paper, metallic gold acrylic paint, and fan paintbrush.

For each stripe, dip tip of paintbrush into paint. Holding paintbrush upright, use a light stamping motion to stamp short diagonal lines across wrapping paper. Painting in opposite direction, paint back across stripe with diagonal lines leaning in opposite direction to form small "X's"; allow to dry.

BRUSHED CELLOPHANE GIFT WRAP
You will need clear cellophane, purple foil wrapping paper, metallic gold acrylic paint, and fan paintbrush.

1. Use paintbrush and broad, curving strokes to paint cellophane; allow to dry.
2. Place painted side of cellophane and right side of wrapping paper together to wrap gift.

SPONGED CELLOPHANE GIFT WRAP
You will need clear cellophane, gold foil wrapping paper, 3 different shades of metallic gold acrylic paint, and 3 pieces of natural sponge.

1. Dampen 1 sponge piece. Using a light stamping motion, use sponge to randomly stamp cellophane with 1 shade of gold paint. Allowing to dry between colors, repeat to stamp cellophane with remaining shades of gold paint.
2. Place painted side of cellophane and right side of wrapping paper together to wrap gift.

TASSEL ORNAMENTS

(Shown on page 60)

For each ornament, you will need one 1½" dia. plastic foam ball, one 7" square each of gold mesh fabric and gold lamé fabric, one 7" square and one 1" x 5½" strip of polyester bonded batting, one 2½" x 5½" strip cut from untwisted metallic purple paper twist, nine 24" lengths cut from gold bead garland, one 5" length and one 10" length of 24-gauge florist wire, one 1" dia. wooden bead, 9" of ³⁄₁₆" dia. gold twisted cord, desired gold trims, metallic gold spray paint, hot glue gun, and glue sticks.

1. Place mesh fabric square wrong side up on a flat surface. Center lamé fabric square wrong side up over mesh fabric square. Center batting square over lamé fabric square. Center plastic foam ball on batting.
2. Gather corners of fabrics and batting together, pulling fabrics taut over ball. Wrap 5" wire length around gathered fabric and batting at base of ball to secure fabric and batting. Trim excess fabric and batting to ½" from ball.
3. Place garland lengths on a flat surface, aligning ends. Use 10" wire length to tightly wire centers of garland lengths together. Glue wired center of garland lengths to excess fabric at base of ball. Trim ends of garland lengths even.
4. Referring to **Fig. 1**, wrap batting strip around base of ball, covering wired center of garland; glue top edge of batting to base of ball. Fold twisted paper strip in half lengthwise. Glue paper strip around base of ball, covering batting strip. Referring to photo, glue desired trims around twisted paper.

Fig. 1

5. For hanger, spray paint bead gold. Fold cord in half to form a loop; glue ends of cord inside bead. Glue bead to top of tassel. Glue desired trim around base of bead.

JEWEL BOX ORNAMENTS (Shown on page 60)

For each ornament, you will need an unfinished wooden box with removable lid (we used 4½"w x 7"l x 3¼"h and 4½"w x 4½"l x 3¼"h boxes), fabric to cover lid, polyester bonded batting, metallic gold spray paint, desired colors of acrylic paint, paintbrushes, jewel stones, gold cord and braid trims, and craft glue.

1. (**Note:** Refer to photo for all steps. Allow to dry after each paint or glue step.) Spray paint inside and outside of box and lid gold. Use acrylic paint to paint bands around box.
2. To cover top of lid, use lid as a pattern to cut a piece of batting. Cut a piece of fabric ¼" larger on all sides than batting piece. Glue batting to top of lid. Center fabric right side up over batting. Alternating sides and pulling fabric taut, glue edges of fabric to sides of lid.
3. Glue cords and trims to box and lid as desired, being sure to cover raw edges of fabric on box lid. Glue jewel stones to box.

CHRISTMAS STAR (Shown on page 59)

You will need one 18" x 27" piece and one 14" square of heavyweight cardboard, metallic gold spray paint, purple acrylic paint, natural sponge piece, gold glitter, craft glue, felt-tip pen, gold twisted cord, 1 purchased flat star-shaped filigree ornament (we used a 7"w gold ornament), desired fabric, and jewel stones.

1. For large star, use pen and a ruler and refer to Diagram A to draw star on 18" x 27" cardboard piece; cut out star. Referring to Diagram B and using 14" cardboard square, repeat for small star.
2. Spray paint both sides of each star gold; allow to dry.
3. For large star, dampen sponge piece. Lightly stamp 1 side (front) of large star with purple paint. While paint is wet, randomly sprinkle glitter over paint. Allow to dry; gently shake off excess glitter.
4. For small star, spread glue on 1 side (front) of star. While glue is wet, sprinkle glitter over glue, covering star completely. Allow to dry; gently shake off excess glitter.
5. Referring to photo, glue large star over small star; allow to dry. Glue lengths of cord from point to point of large star; allow to dry.
6. For star ornament, cut a piece of fabric to cover desired open areas of ornament; glue fabric to back of ornament. Glue jewel stones to front of ornament. Glue ornament to center of large star.

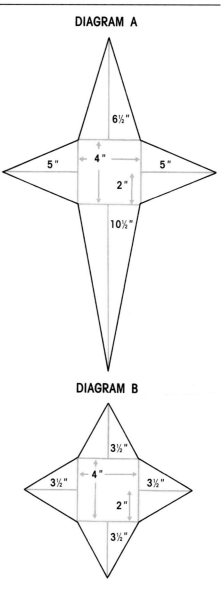

DIAGRAM A

6½"

5" 4" 5"

2"

10½"

DIAGRAM B

3½"

3½" 4" 3½"

2"

3½"

WISE MEN (Shown on page 58)

For each Wise Man, you will need one 12"h x 4" dia. plastic foam cone; 24-gauge florist wire; 16-gauge florist wire; aluminum foil; white, brown, and black acrylic paint; paintbrushes; cosmetic blush; ⅜"w paper-backed fusible web; thread to match fabrics; polyester bonded batting; desired gold decorative cords and braid trims; desired jewel stones; black permanent felt-tip pen with fine point; wire cutters; hot glue gun; glue sticks; and craft glue.

For Gaspar (purple-robed Wise Man), will also need flesh pink Fimo® modeling compound, dark grey wool doll hair, one 14" x 36½" piece of purple fabric for robe and one 5½" x 14" piece of purple fabric for sleeves, one 5" square of blue fabric for headdress, two 4½" x 22½" pieces of gold fabric for scarves, compass, and 15½" of 2"w gold wire mesh ribbon and purchased mini gold pieces for gift.

For Balthazar (gold-robed Wise Man), you will also need terra-cotta Fimo® modeling compound; black curly wool doll hair; one 14" x 36½" piece of gold fabric for robe and one 5½" x 14" piece of gold fabric for sleeves; one 10" square of blue fabric for turban; one 4½" x 28" piece of purple fabric for shawl; and 1 purchased 1½"h miniature brass lamp, metallic gold paint, paintbrush, one 10mm bead cap, one 8mm bell cap, 12" of ⅛"w gold chain, two 5mm jump rings, 3 small gold beads, and metallic gold thread for gift.

For Melchior (fuschia-robed Wise Man), you will also need champagne Fimo® modeling compound; black wool doll hair; one 14" x 36½" piece of fuschia fabric for robe and one 5½" x 14" piece of fuschia fabric for sleeves; one 6" x 11" piece of blue fabric for crown; one 6¾" x 30" piece each of gold fabric and gold mesh fabric for sash; and 1 purchased miniature perfume bottle, metallic gold paint, and paintbrush for gift.

Note: Use craft glue for gluing unless otherwise indicated.

GASPAR

1. To make modeling compound pliable, place modeling compound in a sealable plastic bag in a bowl of warm water for several minutes. Remove from bag and knead.

2. (**Note:** For Steps 2 - 4, use fingers or a craft stick to smooth surface of modeling compound.) Cut an 18" length of 16-gauge wire; fold wire in half. For head, use small strips of aluminum foil to form an inverted egg shape over folded end of wire, making sure egg shape is smooth and firm (**Fig. 1**). Cover aluminum foil with a ⅛" thick layer of modeling compound.

Fig. 1

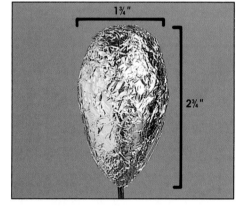

3. (**Note:** Refer to photo, page 58, for Steps 3 and 4. Be careful not to overwork shapes when smoothing.) For brow, form a 1¼" long x ¼" dia. roll from modeling compound. Center roll on head ⅝" below top of head (**Fig. 2a**). For nose, form a ¾" long x ¼" dia. roll. Center roll on head with top of roll touching center of brow (**Fig. 2a**). Smooth edges of rolls onto head, forming brow and nose (**Fig. 2b**). For cheeks, form two ½" dia. balls. Place balls on head below brow (**Fig. 2b**). Smooth balls onto head, forming cheeks (**Fig. 2c**).

Fig. 2a

Fig. 2b

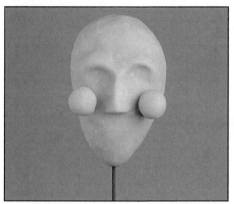

Fig. 2c

4. For each hand, form one 1½" long x ⅜" dia. roll from modeling compound. Flatten 1¼" of 1 end of roll to approx. ¼" thick, forming a paddle shape. Curve paddle into desired hand shape. Use end of 16-gauge wire to make a ½" deep hole in remaining end (wrist end) of hand.

5. Follow manufacturer's instructions to bake head and hands; allow to cool.

6. For eyes, refer to photo and use a pin to lightly etch eye outlines on face. Allowing to dry between colors, paint eyes white, irises brown, pupils black, and highlights white. Outline eyes with black pen. Apply cosmetic blush to cheeks. Trim wire at base of head to 3".

7. For robe, cut one 36½" long piece each from web and 24-gauge wire. Follow manufacturer's instructions to fuse web piece along 1 long edge on wrong side of robe fabric piece. Placing wire in fold of fabric, fold webbed edge of fabric ½" to wrong side; fuse in place.

8. (**Note:** Use a ¼" seam allowance for remaining steps unless otherwise indicated.) Matching right sides and short edges, fold robe fabric piece in half. Sew short edges together to form a tube. Press seam open and turn right side out. Baste ½" and ¼" from remaining raw edge (top) of fabric piece.

9. For sleeves, match right sides and fold sleeve fabric piece in half lengthwise. Sew long edges together to form a tube. Press seam open and turn right side out. Baste ¼" from each remaining raw edge.

10. For arms, cut a 13½" length from 16-gauge wire. Cut a 6" x 12½" piece from batting. Center and hot glue wire length ½" from 1 long edge of batting. Wrap remainder of batting around wire; hot glue to secure. Insert covered wire into sleeves. Hot glue 1 hand in desired position to each end of wire. For each sleeve, pull basting thread, gathering sleeve around wrist; knot thread and trim ends. Arrange and hot glue gathers to wrist. Glue desired trim over gathers, covering raw edge of fabric.

11. (**Note:** Refer to photo for remaining steps.) To assemble Wise Man, place robe over cone with seam at center back and wired edge at bottom. Pull basting threads, gathering robe around top of cone; knot threads and trim ends. Arrange and hot glue gathers to cone. Glue desired trim over gathers, covering raw edge of fabric. To attach head, insert wire at base of head into center top of cone; hot glue to secure. To attach arms, hot glue center of arms to top edge of robe at back of cone. Arrange arms as desired.

12. For beard, cut one 3" to 6" length of hair. Fold length in half; glue fold to face. Repeat for remainder of beard and to cover back of head with hair. For mustache, cut one 3" length of hair. Fold

length in half; glue fold to face below nose. For each eyebrow, cut one 2"l x ¼"w length of hair. Knot length at 1 end; trim short end close to knot. With knot at inner point of brow, glue eyebrow in place; allow to dry. Carefully clip off knot. Arrange and trim hair, beard, mustache, and eyebrows as desired.

13. For headdress, use compass to draw one 4" dia. circle on blue fabric; cut out. Baste ⅛" from edge of circle. Place circle right side up on top of head. Pull basting thread, gathering circle around top of head; knot thread and trim ends. Glue headdress to head to secure. Glue desired trim around base of headdress, covering raw edge of fabric. Glue jewel stones to headdress.

14. For each scarf, press edges of 1 scarf fabric piece ¼" to wrong side; glue to secure. Glue desired trim and jewel stones to scarf. Drape 1 scarf over each shoulder, crossing scarves at back and gluing in place if necessary.

15. For pendant, glue desired trim around edge of a large jewel stone. Glue a smaller jewel stone to trim. Cut one 8½" length of gold cord; knot ends together. Glue knot to back of pendant. Place pendant around neck.

16. For gift, glue desired trims to edges of wire mesh ribbon. Gather ribbon and place in hands; hot glue to secure. Glue jewel stones and gold pieces to ribbon between hands.

BALTHAZAR

1. Follow Steps 1 - 12 of Gaspar instructions, page 66 and this page, to make and assemble Wise Man.

2. For turban, cut a 9"w x 6"h triangle from blue fabric. Press edges of triangle ¼" to wrong side; glue to secure. With wrong side of triangle facing head, center bottom edge of triangle at back of head and wrap bottom points of triangle around head to front. Overlap points on forehead and glue to secure. Fold top point of triangle over head to front, covering bottom points; glue to secure. Tuck and arrange folds of turban around head; glue to secure if necessary. Glue desired trim around edge of jewel stone; glue stone to front of turban.

3. For shawl, press edges of shawl fabric piece ¼" to wrong side; glue to secure. Glue desired trim and jewel stones to shawl. Drape shawl over shoulders,

arranging as desired and gluing in place if necessary.

4. For gift, paint lamp gold; allow to dry. Place bead cap on top of bell cap. Use 1 jump ring to attach eye of bell cap to 1 end of chain. Hot glue bottom of bell cap into opening at top of lamp. Attach remaining jump ring to remaining end of chain. String 1 bead onto a 4" length of gold thread. Thread both ends of thread through remaining beads. Knot ends of thread around jump ring at end of chain and trim ends. Glue jewel stones to lamp. Hot glue chain of lamp into hands.

MELCHIOR

1. Follow Steps 1 - 12 of Gaspar instructions, page 66 and this page, to make and assemble Wise Man.

2. For crown, measure around head; add ½". Cut lengths of desired trims the determined measurement. Glue long edges of trims together to form an approx. 1½" wide length of trim. Glue jewel stones to trim. Overlapping ends ½", glue ends of trim together to form crown shape. Glue desired trim along short edges and 1 long edge on both sides of blue fabric. Baste ¼" from remaining long edge of fabric. Pull basting thread, gathering fabric to same width as back of head. Glue gathered edge of fabric along bottom inside edge of back of crown. Glue crown to head.

3. Glue desired trims around sleeves.

4. For sash, place gold fabric piece right side up. Place mesh fabric piece over gold fabric. Glue edges of fabric pieces together. Glue desired trim along long edges. Baste along each short edge of fabric piece. Pull basting threads, gathering ends of fabric tightly; knot threads and trim ends. Place sash on Wise Man with gathered ends at shoulder; glue in place. Glue desired trims around edge of a jewel stone; glue jewel stone over gathers at shoulder.

5. For gift, paint desired areas of perfume bottle gold; allow to dry. Glue jewel stones to bottle. Hot glue bottle into hands.

CHRISTMAS CAROUSEL

Old-fashioned carousel horses are as enchanting today as they were at the turn of the century. Inspired by their grace and charm, we created a collection filled with romantic images of these fanciful steeds from yesteryear. Rose swags and satin bows echo the pretty pastel trims adorning the prancing horses. Iridescent glass ball ornaments, gold glass icicles, and glittery snowflakes shimmer and sparkle amid tiny white lights. A small mirror at the top of the tree reflects the captivating scene below. At the bottom, a lovely shirred tree skirt is edged with white roses, lace, and satin ribbons. Take a magical ride into the past on this nostalgic Christmas carousel! Instructions for the projects begin on page 74.

Festooned with flowers and ribbons, the lovely **Carousel Horse** (*page 77*) will add a magical touch to your Christmas celebration. *Opposite*: For their dainty dance around the **Christmas Carousel Tree** (*page 74*), **Carousel Horse Ornaments** (*page 74*) are dressed up with embellished saddles, bridles, and reins. Graceful **Ribbon and Rose Swags** (*page 74*) in pastel colors complement their delicate beauty. Draping the base of the tree in soft folds, the **Lace and Roses Tree Skirt** (*page 78*) is edged with Battenberg lace, white roses, and satin ribbons.

The spirited steed on the **Carousel Horse Sweatshirt** (*page 76*) is created with fabric paint and embellished with satin cord, gold trims, ribbon roses, and a satin bow. *Opposite:* The elegant **Painted Cutwork Stockings** (*page 78*) are adorned with a beautiful rose and little buds edged with iridescent paint. The whimsical **Carousel Horse Ornament** (*page 74*) will delight both children and adults.

BUTTON
COUNTRY
CHRISTMAS

The Christmas celebrations of the Early Americans were humble, often featuring homespun decorations crafted from everyday household items. Inspired by their pioneering spirit, we created this charming country collection.

Conveying the simple faith of the settlers, angels crafted from wooden spoons smile from the branches of the tree, surrounded by heart and star ornaments. Muslin yo-yo "icicles" adorned with buttons add a domestic touch, and whimsical blackbirds perch throughout the boughs, from the twig bow at the top to the picket fence where sunflowers are blooming at the base.

A small feather tree trimmed with yo-yo hearts and wooden stars makes a delightful accent for an adjoining room. Hanging from a makeshift clothesline, homey stockings are patched up with fabric scraps, hearts, and buttons. A mason jar lamp filled with colorful buttons is topped with an embellished shade. And the sweet angel on the quilted wall hanging encourages holiday guests to "Be Merry."

With this folksy collection, your Christmas celebration will be filled with down-home charm. Instructions for the projects begin on page 86.

Casting a cheerful light over your Christmas correspondence, the **Button Country Lamp** (*page 88*) is perfect for a desk or chairside table. Handcrafted **Country Cutouts Stationery** (*page 89*) will make your Yuletide greetings extra special. Homespun fabric hearts and trees, buttons and bows, and hand-drawn ''stitches'' adorn the cards. *Opposite*: Echoing the angels and hearts from the tree, the quilted **''Be Merry'' Wall Hanging** (*page 90*) is stitched with a happy Christmas message. A variety of country fabrics and unique buttons adds to its appeal.

In pioneer days, children often hung their socks on the mantel in anticipation of Santa's Christmas Eve visit. With their fabric scrap patches, the **Simple Stockings** (*page 88*) here would have looked right at home next to those from long ago.

Topping the **Button Country Tree** (*page 86*) in perfect style, this twig bow is embellished with colorful buttons and painted wooden stars.

With its wooden dowel trunk and wired garland branches tipped with red beads, this handcrafted **Feather Tree** (*page 87*) will bring a country touch to any room in the house. The **Yo-Yo Heart Ornaments** (*page 87*) and wooden stars decorating the tree are hung from the branches with jute. A Shaker pail is just the right size to hold the little tree.

(*Opposite*) From the twig bow tree topper to the **Picket Fence** (*page 89*) at the bottom, the **Button Country Tree** (*page 86*) has plenty of homespun charm. **Spoon Angels** (*page 86*) and **Wooden Heart Ornaments** (*page 86*) share the tree branches with **Yo-Yo ''Icicles''** (*page 87*) and **Pieced Heart Ornaments** (*page 91*). Little blackbirds with fabric wings and button eyes, a jute garland trimmed with buttons and stars, and wooden bead garlands round out the folksy decorations.

THE SHARING OF CHRISTMAS

With the advent of Christmas, we often experience the same sense of eager anticipation that we knew as children. Thrills like discovering our stockings filled with goodies and packages from Santa are fondly recalled. As the years pass, we find that giving gifts is equally joyful, especially when our offerings have been handcrafted with loving care. The embellished clothing and accessories here can be enjoyed throughout the holidays, making them perfect for early giving. During this special season, these festive gifts will be delightful reminders of the affection we feel for one another.

These festive shirts are sure to receive delighted ooh's and aah's. The three trees on the cross-stitched **Christmas Tree Sweater** (page 110) are trimmed with tiny red beads. The cute country ornaments on the **Trim-a-Tree Sweatshirt** (page 102) are attached to the painted tree with Velcro® brand fasteners. A plaid bow at the bottom is a cheerful finishing touch.

*H*ere's the perfect top to wear to a Yuletide celebration (opposite). The colorful **Poinsettia Blouse** (page 111) is painted with pretty poinsettias and little clusters of holly. Gold buttons and trim add extra flair.

*M*ake the holiday season more fun than ever with these great fashions. Cheery Christmas tree appliqués finished with blanket stitch adorn the stylish **Appliquéd Blazer** (page 106) shown opposite. The jacket is trimmed with coordinating fabrics for a polished look. It's easy to jazz up ready-to-wear vests with merry fabrics and trims. The man in your life can join in the festivities with the bright **Plaid Vest** (page 104). In addition to the distinctive prairie point edging, the delightful **Prairie Points Vest** (page 104) features jaunty star appliqués.

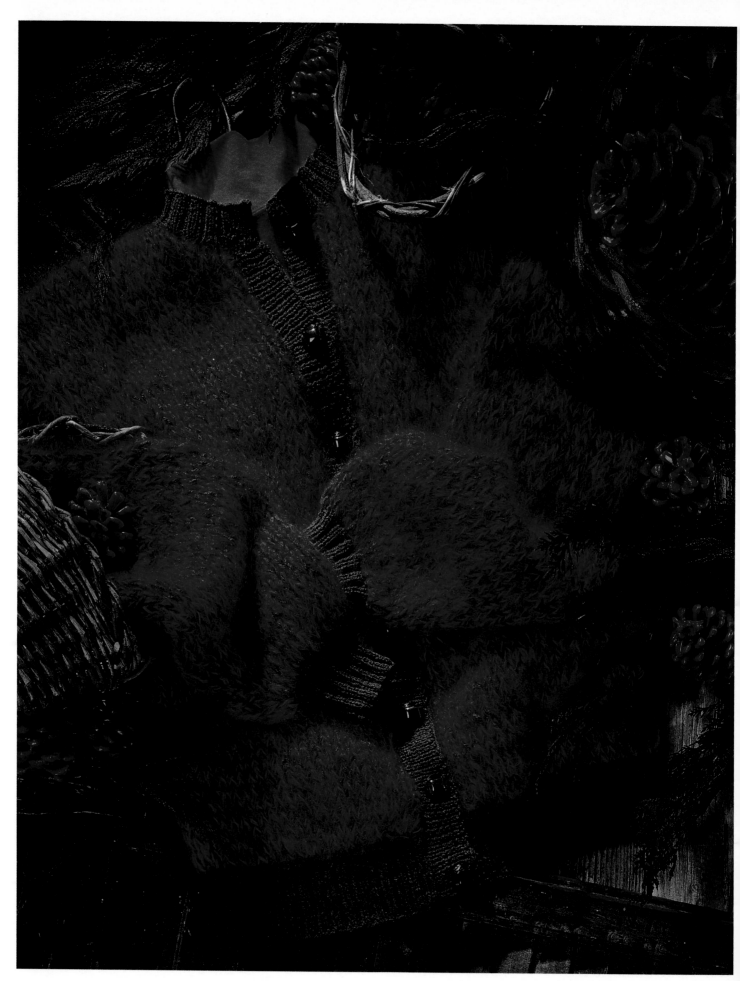

*S*trands of warm, fuzzy mohair
and sport weight yarns are combined
to create the luxurious look and feel
of this knitted **Christmas Cardigan**
(page 108) *worked in seasonal shades
of red and green* (opposite).

*T*hese terrific tops
*for work or play show
plenty of holiday spirit.
Cross-stitched Santa
button covers and
plaid ribbon make the*
Santa Button Blouse
(page 110) *extra special.
Welcoming winter with
outstretched arms, a
row of happy snowmen
adds wintry charm to the
cross-stitched* **Snowman
Tunic** (page 109).

Children will look adorable dressed in these fun holiday fashions. A playful Santa juggles pom-pom snowballs on the whimsical cross-stitched **"Ho-Ho-Ho" Sweatshirt** (page 103). A little one will look "beary" cute in the coordinating **Romper and Shoes** (page 105). Created with fabric paint, the lovable bear and spray of stars express the joy of the season.

The precious **Hearts and Bears Pinafore** (page 107) shown opposite will delight any young miss at Christmastime — or anytime! The pinafore is embellished with eyelet ruffles and heartwarming cross-stitched motifs on the bib and pockets.

You w
white
and
shoel
brow
dime
bottle
black
point,
form
pape

ROMI
1. Wo
to pai
Insert
2. (No
steps
star p
tracin
positi
penci
repea

THE TASTES
OF CHRISTMAS

Drifting from our kitchens during the holidays, the delicious aromas of homemade treats, mingled with spices and fruit, are as inviting as the decorations throughout our homes. With joyful hands and loving hearts, we prepare an array of tempting goodies to share with family and friends. Whether the delectable offerings are packaged and delivered as gifts or served in our own homes, they are a tantalizingly tasteful way to share the spirit of the season.

INTERNATIONAL SAMPLER DINNERS

For a holiday meal with international appeal, offer a sampling of traditional recipes from around the world. You can choose one of our two complete menus — or mix and match your favorite dishes to create your own exciting array of flavors.

Curry-Mushroom Soup	Tortilla Soup
Rack of Lamb with Olive Stuffing	Pork Loin Roast in White Wine
Eggplant Napoleon	Chinese Rice Ring with Broccoli
Green Bean Sauté	English Christmas Cabbage
Tzimmes	Winter Vegetable Trio
Challah	Benne Seed Cookies
Mousse au Chocolate	Chocolate Rum Balls

RACK OF LAMB WITH OLIVE STUFFING

LAMB

- 8 cloves garlic, divided
- 2 tablespoons finely chopped fresh parsley
- 1 tablespoon dried rosemary leaves
- 1 tablespoon olive oil
- 2 racks of lamb (approximately 2 pounds per rack), frenched with fat trimmed to ¼-inch thickness
  Salt and ground black pepper
- 3 tablespoons Dijon-style mustard
- ¼ cup butter or margarine
- ½ cup plain bread crumbs
- 3 cups water

STUFFING

- ¾ cup butter or margarine
- 3 cups coarsely chopped onions
- 1 cup coarsely chopped celery
- 2 tablespoons ground sage
- 2 tablespoons dried rosemary leaves
- 1 tablespoon dried thyme leaves
- 2 teaspoons poultry seasoning
- 1 teaspoon salt
- ½ teaspoon ground black pepper
- 4 cups corn bread crumbs
- 5 slices white bread, torn into small pieces (about 4 cups)
- 1 cup finely chopped green olives
- 1 jar (3½ ounces) capers, drained
- 4 eggs, beaten
- 1 can (14½ ounces) chicken broth

  Fresh rosemary for garnish

For lamb, finely chop 7 cloves of garlic. In a small bowl, combine chopped garlic, parsley, rosemary, and oil. Rub garlic mixture over all sides of lamb. Cover and refrigerate overnight.

For stuffing, preheat oven to 350 degrees. In a large skillet, melt butter over medium heat. Add onions and celery; cook until tender. Remove from heat. In a small food processor, combine sage, rosemary, thyme, poultry seasoning, salt, and pepper; process until mixture is a fine powder. In a large bowl, combine next 4 ingredients and herb mixture. Stir in onion mixture, eggs, and chicken broth.

(Opposite) An impressive addition to your holiday table, tender Rack of Lamb is seasoned with garlic and rosemary. Flavorful Olive Stuffing is the perfect accompaniment to this Greek entrée.

Curry-Mushroom Soup makes a zesty first course with its Indian flavor. Garnished with crispy crumbled bacon, the delicious soup features mushrooms, spinach, and onions.

Spoon into a greased 9 x 13-inch pan, cover, and bake 50 minutes. Uncover and bake 10 minutes longer or until top is golden brown. Remove from oven, cover, and keep warm.

Increase oven temperature to 450 degrees. Sprinkle salt and pepper over all sides of lamb. Heat a large heavy skillet over medium-high heat. Place lamb in skillet, fat side down, and cook until fat is browned. Remove from heat. Place racks of lamb, fat side up, in a shallow roasting pan. Insert meat thermometer into lamb, making sure thermometer does not touch bone or fat. Spread mustard over fat side of lamb. Mince remaining clove of garlic. In same skillet, melt butter over medium heat. Stir garlic into butter and cook until garlic begins to brown. Remove from heat; stir in bread crumbs. Press bread crumb mixture into mustard. Pour water into roasting pan. Cover lamb and roast about 1 hour or until thermometer reaches 175 degrees. Arrange racks of lamb on a serving plate. Fill inside of racks with stuffing. Garnish with fresh rosemary. Slice individual rib sections and serve with additional stuffing.
Yield: 6 to 8 servings

CURRY-MUSHROOM SOUP

- ¾ cup butter or margarine, divided
- 4 cups (about 12 ounces) sliced fresh mushrooms
- 1 cup finely chopped onion
- ⅓ cup all-purpose flour
- 3 tablespoons curry powder
- 2 teaspoons garlic powder
- 2 teaspoons salt
- ½ teaspoon ground black pepper
- 4 cups milk
- 2 cups whipping cream
- 1 package (10 ounces) frozen chopped spinach, thawed and drained
- 6 slices bacon, cooked, drained, and crumbled

In a large skillet, melt ¼ cup butter over medium heat. Add mushrooms and onion; cook until tender. Remove from heat. In a Dutch oven, melt remaining ½ cup butter over medium heat. Stir in flour, curry powder, garlic powder, salt, and pepper. Cook 2 minutes. Whisking constantly, gradually add milk and cream and cook until thickened. Stir in mushroom mixture and spinach. Cook until heated through. To serve, ladle soup into bowls and sprinkle bacon over soup.
Yield: about nine 1-cup servings

Prepared in the French style, this handsome Pork Loin Roast in White Wine is wonderfully moist and tender. The succulent roast is marinated in a mixture of white wine, herbs, and orange juice before cooking.

PORK LOIN ROAST IN WHITE WINE

2 cups dry white wine
¼ cup frozen orange juice concentrate, thawed
½ cup finely chopped fresh parsley
2 teaspoons dried sage
1 teaspoon dried rosemary leaves
3 to 3½ pound pork loin roast on the bone
  Salt and ground black pepper
3 cloves garlic, thinly sliced
3 cups water

Orange slices and fresh parsley for garnish

For marinade, whisk wine, orange juice, parsley, sage, and rosemary in a medium bowl. Sprinkle all sides of roast with salt and pepper. Use a sharp knife to make slits in roast; place garlic slices into slits. Place roast in a 1-gallon resealable plastic bag. Pour marinade over roast. Seal bag and refrigerate 8 hours or overnight, turning several times.

Preheat oven to 350 degrees. Reserving marinade, place roast, fat side up, in a shallow baking pan. Pour water into pan. Insert a meat thermometer into roast, making sure thermometer does not touch bone or fat. Roast about 1½ hours, basting every 30 minutes with marinade. If

necessary, add more wine to marinade.

Reduce oven temperature to 325 degrees. Continue roasting 30 to 40 minutes or until meat thermometer registers 185 degrees and juices run clear when roast is pierced with a fork. Transfer roast to a serving platter and garnish with orange slices and parsley. Let stand 10 minutes before carving. Combine meat drippings and remaining marinade in a small saucepan. Bring to a boil; boil 2 minutes. Spoon a small amount of marinade mixture over each serving of roast.

Yield: about 6 servings

TORTILLA SOUP

6 cans (14½ ounces each) chicken broth
2 cans (4 ounces each) chopped mild green chilies, undrained
⅓ cup fresh mint leaves
2 cloves garlic, minced
1 teaspoon chili powder
1 teaspoon ground cumin seed
1 cup chopped fresh tomatoes
2 avocados, peeled, pitted, and chopped
½ cup chopped fresh cilantro
4 slices bacon, cooked, drained, and crumbled
3 cups coarsely crushed tortilla chips

Sour cream and fresh cilantro for garnish

For soup, combine chicken broth, chilies, mint leaves, garlic, chili powder, and cumin in a Dutch oven. Bring to a boil. Reduce heat to medium, cover, and simmer 1 hour.

While broth is simmering, combine tomatoes, avocados, chopped cilantro, and bacon in a medium bowl; set aside.

Strain broth and return to pan; bring to a boil again.

To serve, spoon about ¼ cup each of avocado mixture and tortilla chips into each bowl. Ladle broth mixture into each bowl. Garnish with sour cream and cilantro. Serve immediately.
Yield: about 12 servings

GREEN BEAN SAUTÉ

¼ cup butter or margarine
1 pound fresh mushrooms, sliced
½ cup finely chopped onion
2 cloves garlic, minced
1 teaspoon salt
½ teaspoon ground black pepper
2 cans (16 ounces each) cut green beans, drained
1 cup (7 ounces) crumbled feta cheese

In a large skillet, melt butter over medium heat. Add mushrooms, onion, garlic, salt, and pepper; cook until mushrooms are tender. Add green beans; cook 5 to 7 minutes or until heated through. Stir in cheese. Serve hot.
Yield: about 10 servings

Chunks of fresh tomato and avocado lend festive color to Mexican Tortilla Soup. Feta cheese, garlic, and fresh mushrooms make our Greek Green Bean Sauté especially savory.

117

For sauce, combine onion, olive oil, and garlic in a large saucepan. Cook over medium heat until onion is tender. Add remaining ingredients; stir until well blended. Bring to a boil, reduce heat to low, cover, and simmer 30 minutes.

While sauce is simmering, peel and coarsely chop 1 eggplant. In a blender or food processor, process chopped eggplant, mushrooms, salt, and pepper until puréed. In a medium skillet, heat olive oil over medium heat. Add eggplant mixture; cook until all liquid has evaporated. Remove eggplant mixture and sauce from heat, cover, and set aside.

Peel and slice remaining 2 eggplants into ¼-inch-thick slices (about 24 slices). In a medium bowl, combine bread crumbs, cheese, and garlic powder. Place flour and eggs in separate small bowls. Dip each slice of eggplant into flour and then egg; coat well with bread crumb mixture. In a large skillet, fry eggplant slices in hot vegetable oil in batches until golden brown on both sides. Transfer to paper towels to drain.

If necessary, rewarm sauce and puréed mixture. To serve, spread puréed mixture between 3 slices of fried eggplant and place on serving plate. Spoon about ¼ cup sauce over eggplant. Garnish with fresh oregano. Serve immediately.
Yield: about 8 servings

WINTER VEGETABLE TRIO

  2 pounds rutabagas, peeled and
      quartered
  2 pounds turnips, peeled and
      quartered
  2 pounds russet potatoes, peeled and
      quartered
  1 cup butter or margarine, softened
  1 cup whipping cream
  2 teaspoons salt
  1 teaspoon ground black pepper

     Shredded Cheddar cheese and
        chopped fresh parsley for garnish

In an 8-quart stockpot, cover rutabagas with salted water. Bring water to a boil and cook 15 minutes. Add turnips, potatoes, and enough water to cover vegetables. Bring to a boil again and cook until vegetables are tender; drain.

Transfer vegetables to a very large bowl. Add butter, cream, salt, and pepper. Using an electric mixer, beat vegetables until light and fluffy. Garnish with cheese and parsley.
Yield: about 16 servings

This tasty Winter Vegetable Trio from Sweden combines potatoes, turnips, and rutabagas for a hearty side dish. Topped with a chunky tomato sauce and fresh oregano, Eggplant Napoleon has spicy Italian flavor.

EGGPLANT NAPOLEON

SAUCE
  ½ cup finely chopped onion
  2 tablespoons olive oil
  1 clove garlic, minced
  1 can (29 ounces) tomato sauce
  1 can (14½ ounces) Italian-style
       stewed tomatoes, chopped
  ½ cup grated Parmesan cheese
  1 teaspoon dried parsley flakes
  1 teaspoon granulated sugar
  ½ teaspoon dried oregano leaves
  ½ teaspoon dried basil leaves
  ½ teaspoon dried thyme
  ½ teaspoon salt
  ¼ teaspoon ground black pepper

EGGPLANT
  3 eggplants, divided
  ½ pound fresh mushrooms
  1 teaspoon salt
  1 teaspoon ground black pepper
  2 tablespoons olive oil
  1 cup plain bread crumbs
  ½ cup grated Parmesan cheese
  ½ teaspoon garlic powder
  ½ cup all-purpose flour
  4 eggs, beaten
     Vegetable oil

     Fresh oregano for garnish

English Christmas Cabbage is simmered in beef broth and lightly sweetened with brown sugar. Pork-fried rice is molded in a ring shape and paired with a spicy mixture of broccoli and onions seasoned with red peppers to create the Chinese Rice Ring with Broccoli.

CHINESE RICE RING WITH BROCCOLI

RICE
Vegetable cooking spray
1 egg, beaten
2 tablespoons vegetable oil
½ cup diced raw pork
½ cup finely chopped fresh mushrooms
½ cup finely chopped green onions
4 cups cooked rice
½ cup drained canned green peas
¼ cup soy sauce

BROCCOLI FILLING
⅛ cup sesame oil
3 dried whole red peppers
2 tablespoons soy sauce
2 tablespoons rice wine vinegar
1 tablespoon granulated sugar
1 teaspoon garlic powder
½ teaspoon ground ginger
8 cups fresh broccoli flowerets
1 onion, thinly sliced

For rice, spray a skillet with cooking spray. Add egg and cook, without stirring, until firm. Place cooked egg on a cutting board and finely chop. In a large skillet, heat vegetable oil over medium-high heat. Add pork, mushrooms, and onions. Stirring constantly, cook 4 to 5 minutes or until pork is cooked. Stir in rice, peas, chopped egg, and soy sauce. Pack hot rice mixture into a 6-cup ring mold sprayed with cooking spray. Cover and place in a 200-degree oven until ready to serve.

For broccoli filling, combine sesame oil and peppers in a large skillet. Cook over medium heat 3 to 4 minutes. Stir in next 5 ingredients. Add broccoli and onion, stirring to coat well. Stirring occasionally, cook until broccoli is tender. Remove from heat; remove peppers. Invert rice ring onto a serving plate and spoon broccoli into center of ring. Serve hot.

Yield: about 12 servings

ENGLISH CHRISTMAS CABBAGE

½ pound bacon
2 cans (14½ ounces each) beef broth
½ cup firmly packed brown sugar
¼ cup apple cider vinegar
2 teaspoons salt
1 teaspoon ground black pepper
3 pounds red cabbage, shredded

In a Dutch oven, cook bacon until crisp. Transfer to paper towels to drain; crumble. Add beef broth, sugar, vinegar, salt, and pepper to bacon drippings in Dutch oven. Cook over medium-high heat, stirring until sugar dissolves and mixture comes to a boil. Add cabbage and bring to a boil. Reduce heat to medium-low, cover, and simmer 30 minutes. Transfer to a serving bowl; sprinkle bacon over cabbage. Serve hot.

Yield: about 16 servings

a floured rolling pin to roll each half into a 9 x 13-inch rectangle. Cut each rectangle lengthwise into 3 equal strips. For each loaf, braid 3 strips of dough together; transfer to a separate baking sheet sprayed with cooking spray. Spray tops of loaves with cooking spray. Let rise in a warm place 1 hour or until doubled in size.

Preheat oven to 350 degrees. In a small bowl, beat remaining egg. Brush loaves with egg. Sprinkle poppy seeds evenly over both loaves. Bake 25 to 30 minutes or until golden brown and bread sounds hollow when tapped. Serve warm.
Yield: 2 loaves bread

MOUSSE AU CHOCOLATE

- 1 package (6 ounces) semisweet chocolate chips
- ¾ cup butter or margarine, cut into pieces
- 1 cup whipping cream, divided
- 5 eggs, separated
- ¼ cup orange-flavored liqueur
- ½ cup granulated sugar
- ½ cup sifted confectioners sugar
- 1 teaspoon orange extract

  Mandarin oranges, well drained, for garnish

Stirring constantly, melt chocolate chips and butter in a large saucepan over low heat. Stir in ¼ cup cream. Place egg yolks in a small bowl. Add about ½ cup chocolate mixture to egg yolks; stir until well blended. Gradually add egg yolk mixture to chocolate mixture, stirring until well blended. Stirring constantly, increase heat to medium and cook 2 minutes. Remove from heat and cool to room temperature. Stir in liqueur.

In a large bowl, beat egg whites until foamy. Gradually add granulated sugar and beat until stiff peaks form. Gently fold egg whites into chocolate mixture in saucepan. Spoon mousse into small serving dishes, loosely cover, and chill until ready to serve.

Place a medium bowl and beaters from an electric mixer in the freezer until well chilled. In chilled bowl, whip remaining ¾ cup cream until soft peaks form. Add confectioners sugar and orange extract; whip until stiff peaks form. Garnish with whipped cream and mandarin oranges.
Yield: about 8 servings

These traditional Jewish dishes are sure to become family favorites. A braided loaf of Challah, a light, crusty bread, is sprinkled with poppy seeds. Spiced with cinnamon, nutmeg, and cloves, Tzimmes is a medley of sweet potatoes, onions, carrots, celery, and prunes.

TZIMMES

- 1 pound sweet potatoes, peeled and cut into ½-inch cubes
- 1 pound carrots, thinly sliced
- 2 cups chopped onions
- 2 ribs celery, chopped
- 1 cup chopped pitted prunes (about 6 ounces)
- ½ cup water
- ¼ cup honey
- 2 tablespoons lemon juice
- 2 teaspoons salt
- 1 teaspoon ground cinnamon
- ½ teaspoon dried grated lemon peel
- ½ teaspoon ground nutmeg
- ¼ teaspoon ground cloves

Preheat oven to 325 degrees. Place potatoes, carrots, onions, celery, and prunes in a greased 9 x 13-inch baking dish. In a small bowl, combine remaining ingredients. Pour honey mixture over vegetables. Cover and bake 1 hour 20 minutes to 1 hour 30 minutes or until potatoes and carrots are tender. Serve hot.
Yield: 10 to 12 servings

CHALLAH

- 2 cups milk
- ½ cup butter or margarine
- ⅓ cup granulated sugar
- 2 packages dry yeast
- 4 eggs, divided
- 8 cups all-purpose flour
- 2 teaspoons salt
  Vegetable cooking spray
- 2 teaspoons poppy seeds

In a medium saucepan, combine milk, butter, and sugar; heat to 115 degrees. Remove from heat. Stir in yeast and cool 10 minutes.

Pour milk mixture into a large bowl. Add 3 eggs; beat until well blended. Add flour and salt; stir until a soft dough forms. Turn onto a lightly floured surface and knead until dough becomes smooth and elastic. Place in a large bowl sprayed with cooking spray, turning once to coat top of dough. Cover and let rise in a warm place (80 to 85 degrees) 1 hour or until doubled in size. Turn dough onto a lightly floured surface and punch down. Divide dough in half. Use

BENNE SEED COOKIES

1 cup (about 5 ounces) sesame seeds
¼ cup butter or margarine, softened
1 cup granulated sugar
1 egg
1 teaspoon lemon juice
1 teaspoon vanilla extract
½ cup all-purpose flour
¼ teaspoon salt
¼ teaspoon baking powder

Preheat oven to 350 degrees. Spread sesame seeds on an ungreased baking sheet. Stirring occasionally, bake 5 to 8 minutes or until golden brown. Cool completely on pan.

In a medium bowl, cream butter and sugar until fluffy. Add egg, lemon juice, and vanilla; stir until well blended. In a small bowl, combine flour, salt, and baking powder. Add dry ingredients to creamed mixture and stir until a soft dough forms. Stir in sesame seeds. Drop teaspoonfuls 1 inch apart onto a heavily greased baking sheet. Bake 6 to 8 minutes or until edges are light brown. Transfer to a wire rack to cool completely. Store in an airtight container.

Yield: about 5 dozen cookies

CHOCOLATE RUM BALLS

2 cups (one 12-ounce package) semisweet chocolate chips, divided
¼ cup sour cream
1 tablespoon honey
¼ teaspoon salt
1¾ cups graham cracker crumbs
1 cup sifted confectioners sugar
¾ cup ground walnuts
½ cup butter or margarine, melted
⅓ cup rum

Combine 1 cup chocolate chips, sour cream, honey, and salt in a small saucepan. Stirring constantly, cook over low heat until smooth. Pour into an 8-inch square pan, cover, and freeze 20 minutes. Shape teaspoonfuls of chocolate mixture into about 36 balls; place on aluminum foil and freeze 10 minutes.

In a blender or food processor, finely grind remaining 1 cup chocolate chips; set aside. In a large bowl, combine cracker crumbs, sugar, walnuts, butter, and rum. Press crumb mixture around each chocolate ball, forming 1½-inch balls. Immediately roll in ground chocolate. Store in an airtight container in refrigerator. Serve chilled.

Yield: about 3 dozen rum balls

Guests will love these after-dinner treats! From France, Mousse au Chocolate combines orange and chocolate flavors. African Benne Seed Cookies are thin, sweet sesame seed wafers, and Jamaican Chocolate Rum Balls are rich and moist.

121

You're Invited!

The holidays are always accompanied by a flurry of parties and other social activities as friends and families gather to share the spirit of the season. In this collection, you'll find the perfect dish to take along to any Christmas celebration. Whether you're invited to an open house or a potluck, a tree-trimming or a caroling party, a cookie swap or an office party, these delicious offerings are sure to be greeted with delighted ooh's and aah's.

These tasty appetizers are just right for a holiday open house. Healthy, low-fat Greek Pizza Squares feature a zippy vegetable mixture topped with two types of cheese. Marinated Shrimp Salad receives its zesty flavor from the savory herbs and spices in the marinade.

GREEK PIZZA SQUARES

CRUST

    2 cups bread flour
    1 cup whole-wheat flour
    1 teaspoon granulated sugar
    1 package dry yeast
    1 teaspoon salt
1 1/3 cups warm water
    1 teaspoon olive oil
       Vegetable cooking spray

TOPPING

       Vegetable cooking spray
    1 can (14 1/2 ounces) Italian-style
       stewed tomatoes, undrained
  1/2 cup chopped onion
  1/2 cup chopped green pepper
    1 teaspoon fennel seeds, crushed
    1 teaspoon garlic powder
    1 teaspoon salt
  1/2 teaspoon ground black pepper
    1 can (2 1/4 ounces) sliced black
       olives, drained
    1 cup fat-free shredded mozzarella
       cheese
    4 ounces feta cheese, crumbled

For crust, combine flours, sugar, yeast, and salt in a large bowl. Add water and oil; stir until a soft dough forms. Turn onto a lightly floured surface and knead until dough becomes smooth and elastic. Place in a large bowl sprayed with cooking spray, turning once to coat top of dough. Cover and let rise in a warm place (80 to 85 degrees) 1 hour or until doubled in size.

For topping, heat a medium skillet sprayed with cooking spray over medium heat. Add tomatoes to skillet and coarsely chop. Add onion, green pepper, fennel seeds, garlic powder, salt, and pepper to tomatoes. Stirring occasionally, cook 5 minutes or until liquid evaporates. Remove from heat; stir in olives.

Preheat oven to 375 degrees. Turn dough onto a lightly floured surface and punch down. Press dough into a greased 10 x 15-inch jellyroll pan. Bake 10 minutes. Remove from oven. Spoon tomato mixture over crust. Sprinkle cheeses over vegetable mixture. Bake 15 to 20 minutes or until cheese is bubbly. Cut into squares and serve warm.

Yield: about 2 dozen appetizers

1 serving (2 x 3-inch piece): 88 calories, 2.0 gms fat, 4.5 gms protein, 13.5 gms carbohydrate

The extra crunch in our Crunchy Coleslaw comes from almonds, sunflower kernels, and crushed ramen noodles. Red wine vinegar is the surprise ingredient in the sweet, tangy dressing.

CRUNCHY COLESLAW

    6 cups shredded cabbage
  3/4 cup shredded carrots
    6 green onions, chopped
  1/2 cup sliced almonds
  1/2 cup lightly salted roasted sunflower
       kernels
    1 package (3 ounces) chicken-
       flavored ramen noodle soup mix
  1/4 cup vegetable oil
    2 tablespoons granulated sugar
    2 tablespoons red wine vinegar
  1/2 teaspoon salt
  1/2 teaspoon ground black pepper

In a large bowl, combine cabbage, carrots, onions, almonds, and sunflower kernels. In a small bowl, whisk seasoning packet from ramen noodles and remaining ingredients except noodles. Pour oil mixture over cabbage mixture; stir until well coated. Crush ramen noodles and stir into cabbage mixture. Serve immediately.

Yield: about 7 cups coleslaw

MARINATED SHRIMP SALAD

  1/2 cup white wine vinegar
  1/3 cup olive oil
    6 green onions, chopped
    3 tablespoons chopped fresh parsley
    1 tablespoon garlic salt
    2 teaspoons dried basil leaves, crushed
  1/2 teaspoon ground black pepper
1 1/2 pounds large shrimp, cooked,
       peeled, and deveined
  1/2 red onion, thinly sliced

In a blender or food processor, process vinegar, oil, onions, parsley, garlic salt, basil, and pepper until well blended. In a medium bowl, combine shrimp and red onion. Pour vinegar mixture over shrimp mixture; stir until well coated. Cover and refrigerate 8 hours or overnight to allow flavors to blend. Serve chilled.

Yield: about 4 cups salad

This delightful Chicken-Black Bean Casserole will bring a taste of the Southwest to a holiday potluck. Sprinkled with Parmesan cheese, Peppered Cheese Buns feature a flavorful combination of spices and mellow Romano cheese.

CHICKEN-BLACK BEAN CASSEROLE

⅔ cup lime juice
⅓ cup olive oil
½ teaspoon ground black pepper
2 teaspoons garlic powder, divided
2 teaspoons salt, divided
1½ pounds boneless, skinless chicken breasts, cut into bite-size pieces
4 cups cooked rice
2 cans (15 ounces each) black beans, undrained
1 cup finely chopped fresh cilantro
1 teaspoon onion powder
1 teaspoon chili powder
1 teaspoon ground cumin seeds

In a medium bowl, whisk lime juice, oil, pepper, and 1 teaspoon each garlic powder and salt. Add chicken; stir until evenly coated. Cover and refrigerate 2 hours.

In a 2-quart casserole, combine rice, beans, cilantro, onion powder, chili powder, cumin, and remaining 1 teaspoon each garlic powder and salt; set aside.

Preheat oven to 350 degrees. Using a slotted spoon, place chicken in a large skillet. Cook over medium heat until juices run clear when chicken is pierced with a fork. Stir chicken into rice mixture. Cover and bake 40 to 45 minutes or until heated through.

Yield: about nine 1-cup servings

PEPPERED CHEESE BUNS

1 package dry yeast
1 cup warm water
3 cups all-purpose flour
½ cup grated Romano cheese
2 tablespoons granulated sugar
1 teaspoon garlic powder
1 teaspoon onion powder
1 teaspoon ground black pepper
½ teaspoon salt
1 tablespoon olive oil
Vegetable cooking spray
Grated Parmesan cheese

In a small bowl, combine yeast and water; stir until yeast dissolves. In a medium bowl, combine flour, Romano cheese, sugar, garlic powder, onion powder, pepper, and salt. Add yeast mixture and oil to dry ingredients. Stir until a soft dough forms. Turn onto a lightly floured surface and knead about 5 minutes or until dough becomes smooth and elastic. Place in a medium bowl sprayed with cooking spray, turning once to coat top of dough. Cover and let rise in a warm place (80 to 85 degrees) 1 hour or until doubled in size. Turn dough onto a lightly floured surface and punch down. For each bun, shape about 3 tablespoons dough into a 4-inch-long roll. Tie each roll into a knot and place on a greased baking sheet. Spray tops of buns with cooking spray, cover, and let rise in a warm place 30 minutes or until doubled in size.

Preheat oven to 375 degrees. Bake 12 to 15 minutes or until golden brown. Transfer to a wire rack. Lightly spray buns with cooking spray; sprinkle with Parmesan cheese. Allow to cool completely. Store in an airtight container.

Yield: about 3½ dozen buns

HONEY-WALNUT CRUNCH

1½ cups granulated sugar
½ cup honey
½ cup corn syrup
¼ cup water
1 cup chopped walnuts
2 tablespoons butter or margarine
1 teaspoon lemon extract
½ teaspoon salt
½ teaspoon baking soda

Butter sides of a large heavy saucepan. Combine sugar, honey, corn syrup, and water in pan. Stirring constantly, cook over medium-low heat until sugar dissolves. Using a pastry brush dipped in hot water, wash down any sugar crystals on sides of pan. Attach candy thermometer to pan, making sure thermometer does not touch bottom of pan. Increase heat to medium and bring to a boil. Cook, without stirring, until syrup reaches hard crack stage (approximately 300 to 310 degrees) and turns light golden in color. Test about ½ teaspoon syrup in ice water. Syrup should form brittle threads in ice water and remain brittle when removed from the water. Remove from heat; stir in walnuts, butter, lemon extract, and salt; stir until butter melts. Add baking soda (syrup will foam); stir until soda dissolves. Pour candy onto a large piece of buttered aluminum foil. Using 2 greased spoons, pull edges of warm candy until stretched thin. Cool completely. Break into pieces. Store in an airtight container.
Yield: about 1½ pounds candy

CREAMY WHITE FUDGE

3 cups granulated sugar
1 cup sour cream
⅓ cup light corn syrup
2 tablespoons butter or margarine
¼ teaspoon salt
2 teaspoons vanilla extract
1 cup chopped walnuts

Butter sides of a large heavy saucepan or Dutch oven. Combine sugar, sour cream, corn syrup, butter, and salt in pan. Stirring constantly, cook over medium-low heat until sugar dissolves. Using a pastry brush dipped in hot water, wash down any sugar crystals on sides of pan. Attach candy thermometer to pan, making sure thermometer does not touch bottom of pan. Increase heat to medium and bring to a boil. Cook, without stirring, until syrup reaches soft ball stage (approximately 234 to 240 degrees). Test about ½ teaspoon syrup in ice water. Syrup should easily form a ball in ice water but

Tempting treats for a caroling party include Honey-Walnut Crunch, Creamy White Fudge, and Chocolate-Cream Cheese Cake. Hot Buttered Rum Cordial is a warming blend of cider, rum, and amaretto.

flatten when held in your hand. Place pan in 2 inches of cold water in sink. Add vanilla; do not stir until syrup cools to approximately 200 degrees. Using medium speed of an electric mixer, beat until thickened and no longer glossy. Stir in walnuts. Pour into a buttered 7 x 11-inch baking pan. Cool completely. Cut into 1-inch squares. Store in an airtight container in refrigerator.
Yield: about 5 dozen pieces fudge

HOT BUTTERED RUM CORDIAL

2 cups apple cider
½ cup firmly packed brown sugar
¼ teaspoon ground cinnamon
¼ teaspoon ground allspice
2 cups rum
¼ cup amaretto
1 tablespoon butter-flavored extract

In a small saucepan, combine first 4 ingredients. Stirring constantly, cook over medium heat until sugar dissolves. Remove from heat. Stir in rum, amaretto, and butter-flavored extract. Store in an airtight container in refrigerator 8 hours or overnight to allow flavors to blend. Strain cordial through cheesecloth or a coffee filter. Reheat cordial; serve hot.
Yield: about eighteen 2-ounce servings

CHOCOLATE-CREAM CHEESE CAKE

1 box (18.25 ounces) devil's food cake mix without pudding mix
4 eggs, divided
½ cup butter or margarine, softened
3½ cups sifted confectioners sugar
1 package (8 ounces) cream cheese, softened

For cake, preheat oven to 350 degrees. In a large bowl, combine cake mix, 2 eggs, and butter; beat 2 minutes. Spread batter in a greased and floured 9 x 13-inch glass baking dish. In a small bowl, beat remaining 2 eggs, sugar, and cream cheese until smooth. Spread over cake batter. Bake 35 to 40 minutes or until cake begins to pull away from sides of pan. Cool completely on a wire rack. Store in an airtight container.
Yield: about 12 servings

STAR AND TREE BUTTER COOKIES

COOKIES
    1 cup butter or margarine, softened
1½ cups granulated sugar
    1 egg
    1 teaspoon vanilla extract
2¾ cups all-purpose flour
    ¼ teaspoon salt

ICING
3¾ cups sifted confectioners sugar
    ½ cup plus 1 tablespoon milk
    ½ teaspoon almond extract
      Green paste food coloring
      Purchased white, green, and red
        decorating icing
      Red cinnamon candies
      Purchased red sugar

For cookies, preheat oven to 375 degrees. In a large bowl, cream butter and sugar until fluffy. Add egg and vanilla; stir until smooth. In a small bowl, combine flour and salt. Add dry ingredients to creamed mixture; stir until a soft dough forms. On a lightly floured surface, use a floured rolling pin to roll dough to ¼-inch thickness. Use desired tree- and star-shaped cookie cutters to cut out cookies. Transfer tree- and star-shaped cookies to separate greased baking sheets. Bake tree-shaped cookies 8 to 10 minutes and star-shaped cookies 6 to 8 minutes or until edges are light brown. Transfer cookies to a wire rack with waxed paper underneath to cool completely.

For icing, combine sugar, milk, and almond extract in a small bowl; stir until smooth. Tint green. Ice some of the tree-shaped cookies green. Allow icing to harden. Refer to photo and use a small round tip to pipe white decorating icing onto green-iced tree-shaped cookies for snow. Use a small amount of white icing to secure a red candy to top of each tree. Allow icing to harden. Refer to photo and use a small round tip to pipe green decorating icing onto remaining tree-shaped cookies. Press a red candy on top of each cookie. Allow icing to harden.

Refer to photo and use a small round tip to pipe red icing onto star-shaped cookies. Before icing hardens, sprinkle red sugar on star-shaped cookies. Shake off excess sugar. Allow icing to harden. Store in an airtight container.
Yield: about 3½ dozen 3- to 5-inch cookies

Baked in festive shapes and colorfully decorated, Star and Tree Butter Cookies and Reindeer Cookies make fun additions to a Christmas cookie swap.

REINDEER COOKIES

½ cup butter or margarine, softened
½ cup granulated sugar
½ teaspoon vanilla extract
½ teaspoon almond extract
1⅓ cups all-purpose flour
½ cup finely ground walnuts
¼ teaspoon salt
Purchased white decorating icing
Red cinnamon candies

Trace reindeer pattern onto tracing paper; cut out. Preheat oven to 350 degrees. In a large bowl, cream butter and sugar until fluffy. Add extracts; stir until smooth. In a small bowl, combine flour, walnuts, and salt. Add dry ingredients to creamed mixture; stir until a soft dough forms. On a lightly floured surface, use a floured rolling pin to roll dough to ¼-inch thickness. Place pattern on dough and cut out cookies. Transfer to a greased baking sheet. Bake 8 to 10 minutes or until edges are light brown. Cool on pan 2 minutes. Transfer to a wire rack to cool completely. Refer to photo and use a small round tip to pipe icing onto cookies. Use a small amount of icing to secure red candies on cookies for noses. Allow icing to harden. Store in an airtight container.
Yield: about 1 dozen cookies

For a tree-trimming party, take along these quick-to-fix treats. Chewy Sesame Candy has a deliciously different taste. Coconut and pecans lend extra appeal to delectable Fudge Meltaways. Microwave Caramel Corn is a great, fat-free snack.

FUDGE MELTAWAYS

¾ cup butter or margarine, divided
3 ounces unsweetened baking chocolate, chopped and divided
1½ cups finely crushed vanilla wafers
1 cup sweetened shredded coconut
½ cup chopped pecans
¼ cup granulated sugar
1 egg
2 teaspoons vanilla extract, divided
2 cups sifted confectioners sugar
3 tablespoons milk

Preheat oven to 350 degrees. Stirring constantly, melt ½ cup butter and 1 ounce chocolate in a large saucepan over low heat. Remove from heat; stir in next 5 ingredients and 1 teaspoon vanilla. Press into a buttered 7 x 11-inch baking pan. Bake 8 minutes. Cool completely.

Stirring constantly, melt remaining ¼ cup butter and 2 ounces chocolate in a medium saucepan over low heat. Remove from heat; stir in confectioners sugar, milk, and remaining 1 teaspoon vanilla. Spread over crumb mixture in pan. Cool completely. Cut into 1-inch squares.
Yield: about 5 dozen candies

MICROWAVE CARAMEL CORN

Vegetable cooking spray
16 cups popped popcorn, popped without fat or salt
1 cup firmly packed brown sugar
2 tablespoons light corn syrup
2 tablespoons molasses
½ teaspoon salt
½ teaspoon baking soda
½ teaspoon vanilla extract

Spray inside of a 14 x 20-inch oven cooking bag with cooking spray. Place popcorn in bag. In a 2-quart microwave-safe bowl, combine next 3 ingredients. Microwave on high power (100%) 2 minutes or until mixture boils. Stir and microwave on high power 2 minutes longer. Stir in remaining ingredients. Pour syrup over popcorn; stir and shake until well coated. Microwave on high power 1½ minutes. Stir, shake, and microwave 1½ minutes longer. Spread on aluminum foil sprayed with cooking spray. Cool completely. Store in an airtight container.
Yield: about 16 cups caramel corn

1 serving (1 cup caramel corn):
90 calories, 0 gms fat, 1.0 gms protein, 21.8 gms carbohydrate

SESAME CANDY

1 cup sesame seeds, divided
1 cup old-fashioned rolled oats
1 cup sifted confectioners sugar
¾ cup nonfat dry milk
¾ cup smooth peanut butter
½ cup honey
2 tablespoons water
1 teaspoon vanilla extract

Preheat oven to 350 degrees. Spread sesame seeds on an ungreased baking sheet. Bake 5 to 8 minutes or until light brown. Cool completely on pan.

In a medium bowl, combine ¼ cup sesame seeds and remaining ingredients, stirring until well blended. Shape into 1-inch balls. Roll in remaining sesame seeds. Cover and refrigerate.
Yield: about 6 dozen pieces candy

Here's the perfect combination for a child's school party! The yummy Hoagie Sandwich features ham, turkey, cheese, lettuce, and tomato in a wreath of hearty Oatmeal Bread. Scrumptious chocolate Santa Cupcakes are decorated with icing, candied cherries, and raisins to resemble the jolly old gent's cheerful face.

HOAGIE SANDWICH

1 Oatmeal Bread Wreath (recipe this page)
   Mayonnaise and/or mustard
½ pound thinly sliced cooked ham
½ pound thinly sliced cooked turkey
6 ounces thinly sliced Cheddar cheese
   Sliced tomatoes
   Lettuce
   Sweet red pepper
   Fresh mint leaves

Slice loaf of bread in half horizontally. If desired, spread mayonnaise and/or mustard over each half of bread. Layer ham, turkey, cheese, tomato, and lettuce on bottom half of bread. Replace top of bread. Use sharp knife to cut small round pieces of red pepper for berries. Use a small amount of mayonnaise or mustard to secure mint leaves and red pepper pieces to top of sandwich to resemble holly leaves and berries. Cover and refrigerate until ready to serve.
Yield: 10 to 12 servings

OATMEAL BREAD WREATHS

2 cups water
1 cup old-fashioned rolled oats
6 cups all-purpose flour
½ cup nonfat dry milk
2½ teaspoons salt
2 packages dry yeast
⅓ cup warm water
⅓ cup molasses
¼ cup vegetable oil
   Vegetable cooking spray

In a medium saucepan, bring 2 cups water to a boil. Remove from heat; stir in oats. Cool to room temperature.

In a large bowl, combine flour, dry milk, and salt. In a small bowl, dissolve yeast in ⅓ cup warm water. Add oats mixture, yeast mixture, molasses, and oil to dry ingredients. Stir until a soft dough forms. Turn onto a lightly floured surface and knead until dough becomes smooth and elastic. Place in a large bowl sprayed with cooking spray, turning once to coat top of dough. Cover and let rise in a warm place (80 to 85 degrees) 1 hour or until doubled

in size. Turn dough onto a lightly floured surface and punch down. Divide dough into thirds. Shape each piece of dough into a ball, make a hole in center of dough, and place in a greased 9- or 10-inch tube pan. Spray top of dough with cooking spray, cover, and let rise in a warm place 1 hour or until doubled in size.

Preheat oven to 350 degrees. Bake 25 to 30 minutes or until bread sounds hollow when tapped. Remove from pan and cool completely on a wire rack. Store in an airtight container.
Yield: 3 loaves bread

SANTA CUPCAKES

CUPCAKES

- ½ cup butter or margarine, softened
- ¾ cup firmly packed brown sugar
- 2 eggs
- 1 teaspoon vanilla extract
- 1 cup milk
- ½ cup frozen apple juice concentrate, thawed
- 2¼ cups all-purpose flour
- ½ cup cocoa
- ¾ teaspoon baking soda
- ½ teaspoon salt

FROSTING

- ¾ cup butter or margarine, softened
- 6¾ cups sifted confectioners sugar
- ½ cup milk
- 1 teaspoon vanilla extract
  Red paste food coloring
  Candied cherries, halved
  Raisins

For cupcakes, preheat oven to 375 degrees. In a large bowl, cream butter and sugar until fluffy. Add eggs and vanilla; stir until smooth. Stir in milk and apple juice. In a small bowl, combine flour, cocoa, baking soda, and salt. Add dry ingredients to creamed mixture; stir until well blended. Spoon batter into a paper-lined muffin pan, filling each tin ¾ full. Bake 18 to 20 minutes or until a toothpick inserted in center of cake comes out clean. Transfer to a wire rack to cool completely.

For frosting, combine butter, sugar, milk, and vanilla; stir until smooth. Transfer 1 cup frosting to a small bowl; tint red. Spread a thin layer of white frosting over tops of cupcakes. Refer to photo and press cherries and raisins into frosting for faces. Transfer red and remaining white frostings to separate pastry bags fitted with large star tips. Pipe red frosting onto cupcakes for caps. Pipe white frosting onto cupcakes for trims and beards. Store in an airtight container.

Yield: about 1½ dozen cupcakes

PINEAPPLE CREAM CANDY

- 1 cup granulated sugar
- ½ cup firmly packed brown sugar
- ½ cup crushed pineapple, undrained
- 1 cup chopped walnuts
- 12 large marshmallows
- 1 teaspoon lemon extract

Your coworkers at the office will be delighted by these party treats. Two luscious layers make Chocolate-Butterscotch Candy extra special. Rich Pineapple Cream Candy is a sweet blend of pineapple, marshmallows, and walnuts.

Butter sides of a 2-quart heavy saucepan. Combine sugars and pineapple in pan. Stirring constantly, cook over medium-low heat until sugars dissolve. Using a pastry brush dipped in hot water, wash down any sugar crystals on sides of pan. Attach candy thermometer to pan, making sure thermometer does not touch bottom of pan. Increase heat to medium and bring to a boil. Cook, without stirring, until syrup reaches 200 degrees. Stir in walnuts. Continue to cook until syrup reaches soft ball stage (approximately 234 to 240 degrees). Test about ½ teaspoon syrup in ice water. Syrup should easily form a ball in ice water but flatten when held in your hand. Remove from heat; add marshmallows (do not stir). When marshmallows start to melt, add lemon extract and stir until mixture begins to thicken. Quickly drop tablespoonfuls 1 inch apart onto buttered aluminum foil. Cool completely. Store in an airtight container.

Yield: about 3 dozen pieces candy

CHOCOLATE-BUTTERSCOTCH CANDY

- 1 package (12 ounces) butterscotch-flavored chips
- 1 package (12 ounces) semisweet chocolate chips
- ½ cup raisins
- ½ cup chopped pecans

Line a 7 x 11-inch pan with waxed paper. In separate small saucepans, melt butterscotch and chocolate chips over low heat, stirring constantly. Remove from heat. Stir raisins into butterscotch chips; spread into prepared pan. Stir pecans into chocolate chips; spread over butterscotch mixture. Allow candy to harden. Cut into 1-inch squares. Store in an airtight container in a cool, dry place.

Yield: about 5 dozen pieces candy

CHRISTMAS "LIGHTS"

One of the joys of the holiday season is sharing food, fun, and fellowship with our friends and family. We delight in planning and preparing tempting assortments of delicious foods for these celebrations. This year, why not offer low-calorie, low-fat, and heart-healthy party fare? Your guests will never guess the difference! We've even included nutrition information with each recipe to show you just how healthful it is. These tasty Christmas "lights" are sure to be the bright spot of the festivities!

SHRIMP SALSA

2½ pounds shrimp, cooked, peeled, deveined, and chopped (about 5 cups)
1 jar (24 ounces) mild chunky-style salsa
2 cups chopped fresh cilantro
2 cups finely chopped fresh tomatoes
¼ cup finely chopped red onion
2 tablespoons lime juice

Purchased fat-free tortilla chips to serve

In a large bowl, combine all ingredients. Cover and refrigerate 8 hours or overnight to allow flavors to blend. Serve with tortilla chips.
Yield: about 8 cups salsa or 32 servings

1 serving (¼ cup salsa): 53 calories, 1.1 gms fat, 8.6 gms protein, 2.6 gms carbohydrate

BASIL-DILL CHEESE BALL

2 cups (8 ounces) finely shredded farmer cheese
1 cup fat-free cottage cheese
½ cup finely chopped green onions
¼ cup grated Parmesan cheese
1 tablespoon dried basil leaves, crushed
2 teaspoons dill weed
Chopped fresh cilantro

Crackers to serve

In a medium bowl, combine first 6 ingredients. Shape into a ball. Wrap in plastic wrap and refrigerate 8 hours or overnight to allow flavors to blend. Roll cheese ball in cilantro leaves. To serve, let stand at room temperature 20 to 30 minutes or until softened. Serve with crackers.
Yield: 1 cheese ball or 32 servings

1 serving (1 tablespoon cheese ball): 29 calories, 1.2 gms fat, 3.2 gms protein, 0.7 gms carbohydrate

(Opposite) Quick and easy to prepare, zesty Shrimp Salsa is bursting with flavor. Served with fat-free tortilla chips, the zippy appetizer is a delightful low-calorie treat.

A delicious addition to a holiday buffet, Basil-Dill Cheese Ball is a savory combination of herbs and cheeses. Piquant Salmon Pâté is spiced with horseradish, garlic, onion, and dill weed.

SALMON PÂTÉ

1 container (16 ounces) plain fat-free yogurt
1 can (7½ ounces) skinless red salmon, drained and bones removed
1 cup (4 ounces) shredded fat-free Cheddar cheese
¼ cup fat-free honey Dijon mustard salad dressing
2 teaspoons prepared horseradish
½ teaspoon dried dill weed
½ teaspoon garlic powder
½ teaspoon salt
¼ teaspoon ground black pepper
¼ teaspoon onion powder

Fresh dill weed for garnish
Crackers or cucumber slices to serve

Line a wire strainer with cheesecloth or a coffee filter and place strainer over a medium bowl. Spoon yogurt into strainer. Cover with plastic wrap and refrigerate 24 hours to drain. Discard liquid.
In a medium bowl, combine yogurt solids and next 9 ingredients; stir until well blended. Cover and refrigerate until well chilled. Shape into about a 9-inch-long roll. Garnish with fresh dill weed. Serve with crackers or cucumber slices.
Yield: about 2 cups pâté or 8 servings

1 serving (¼ cup pâté): 102 calories, 1.7 gms fat, 12.5 gms protein, 7.5 gms carbohydrate

CHICKEN PUFFS

PUFFS

- 1 cup all-purpose flour
- 1 teaspoon garlic powder
- ½ teaspoon salt
- ⅛ teaspoon ground red pepper
- 1 cup water
- 2 tablespoons reduced-calorie margarine
- 3 eggs
  Vegetable cooking spray

FILLING

- 2 tablespoons reduced-calorie margarine
- 1 cup evaporated skim milk, divided
- 2 tablespoons all-purpose flour
- ½ teaspoon salt
- ½ teaspoon ground black pepper
- 2 cans (5 ounces each) chicken, drained
- ½ cup peeled diced cucumber
- ¼ cup chopped green onions
- 2 tablespoons white cooking wine

For puffs, preheat oven to 400 degrees. In a small bowl, combine flour, garlic powder, salt, and pepper; set aside.

In a medium saucepan, combine water and margarine. Bring to a boil. Reduce heat to low and gradually stir in flour mixture. Stirring constantly, cook until mixture begins to pull away from sides of pan. Remove from heat; cool 5 minutes. Using high speed of an electric mixer, add eggs, one at a time, beating well after each addition. Drop heaping tablespoonfuls of batter onto a baking sheet sprayed with cooking spray, mounding each spoonful slightly in center. Bake 18 to 20 minutes or until golden brown and puffy. Transfer to a wire rack to cool completely.

For filling, melt margarine in a medium saucepan over medium heat. Stirring constantly, add 2 tablespoons milk, flour, salt, and pepper; cook 2 minutes. Stirring constantly, gradually add remaining milk; cook until thickened. Stir in chicken, cucumber, onions, and wine. Cook about 2 minutes or until heated through. Using a sharp knife, carefully slice tops off puffs. Spoon about 1 tablespoon filling onto bottom halves of puffs; replace tops. Serve warm.

Yield: about 2 dozen puffs

1 serving (1 puff): 68 calories, 2.1 gms fat, 5.9 gms protein, 5.8 gms carbohydrate

Chunks of ham, green onion, and jalapeño pepper add hearty flavor to Hot Spinach Dip. Chicken Puffs filled with a delectable mixture of chicken, cucumber, and green onion are tasty little morsels.

HOT SPINACH DIP

- 1 package (10 ounces) frozen chopped spinach, thawed and well drained
- ½ pound cooked ham, diced
- 1 cup (4 ounces) shredded fat-free mozzarella cheese
- ½ cup fat-free sour cream
- 3 ounces fat-free cream cheese, softened
- ¼ cup chopped green onions
- 1 tablespoon prepared horseradish
- 1 fresh jalapeño pepper, seeded and minced
- 1 teaspoon salt
- ½ teaspoon ground black pepper
  Vegetable cooking spray

Fat-free sour cream and green onion for garnish
Pita bread, cut in wedges, to serve

Preheat oven to 375 degrees. In a large bowl, combine first 10 ingredients. Spread mixture into a 9-inch pie plate sprayed with cooking spray. Bake 15 to 18 minutes or until heated through. Garnish with sour cream and green onion. Serve warm with pita bread.

Yield: about 3 cups dip or 9 servings

1 serving (⅓ cup dip): 85 calories, 1.5 gms fat, 13.6 gms protein, 3.2 gms carbohydrate

Flaky pastry wrappers encase shrimp and a creamy filling to create these wonderful Shrimp Bundles. Light and cool Cucumber Dip is paired with fresh vegetables to make a colorful appetizer.

CUCUMBER DIP

- 1 large cucumber, peeled and cut into quarters
- 1 container (8 ounces) fat-free cottage cheese
- ¼ cup chopped pecans
- 1 teaspoon lemon juice
- 1 package (1 ounce) fat-free ranch salad dressing mix
- 2 tablespoons fat-free mayonnaise
- 1 teaspoon garlic powder
- 1 teaspoon onion powder

    Carrot and fresh parsley for garnish
    Fresh vegetables to serve

In a blender or food processor, combine all ingredients; process until cucumber and pecans are finely chopped. Cover and refrigerate until well chilled. Garnish with carrot and parsley. Serve with fresh vegetables.
Yield: about 2 cups dip or 16 servings

1 serving (2 tablespoons dip): 33 calories, 1.2 gms fat, 1.9 gms protein, 4.0 gms carbohydrate

SHRIMP BUNDLES

- 1 package (8 ounces) fat-free cream cheese, softened
- ¼ cup cooking sherry
- ¼ cup finely chopped green onions
- 1 teaspoon dried tarragon leaves, crushed
- ½ teaspoon garlic powder
- ½ teaspoon salt
- ½ teaspoon ground black pepper
- 9 sheets frozen phyllo pastry, thawed according to package directions
    Olive oil cooking spray
- 3 dozen medium shrimp, cooked, peeled, and deveined (about 1 pound)

Preheat oven to 375 degrees. In a medium bowl, combine cream cheese, sherry, onions, tarragon, garlic powder, salt, and pepper; stir until well blended. Lightly spray each sheet of phyllo pastry with cooking spray. Stack 3 sheets of pastry on top of each other; cut into twelve 4-inch squares. Spoon a heaping teaspoonful of cheese mixture in center of each pastry square. Place 1 shrimp over cheese mixture. Bring corners of pastry squares together and twist. Place on a baking sheet sprayed with cooking spray. Lightly spray each bundle with cooking spray. Repeat with remaining pastry sheets, cheese mixture, and shrimp. Bake 6 to 8 minutes or until light brown. Serve warm.
Yield: about 3 dozen shrimp bundles

1 serving (1 shrimp bundle): 38 calories, 0.2 gms fat, 4.3 gms protein, 4.0 gms carbohydrate

SCALLOPS AND PROSCIUTTO

10 ounces thinly sliced prosciutto
 2 pounds sea scallops
 1 cup lemon juice
¼ cup honey
¼ cup soy sauce
 4 cloves garlic, minced
 2 teaspoons dried tarragon leaves,
       crushed
 1 teaspoon salt
½ teaspoon ground black pepper
   Olive oil cooking spray
 2 teaspoons cornstarch
 2 teaspoons water

Cut prosciutto into ½ x 4-inch strips. Wrap each scallop with 1 strip of prosciutto and secure with a toothpick. In a medium bowl, combine lemon juice, honey, soy sauce, garlic, tarragon, salt, and pepper. Add scallops, cover, and refrigerate 8 hours or overnight to allow flavors to blend.

Spray a large skillet with cooking spray. Heat skillet over medium heat. Reserving lemon juice mixture, use a slotted spoon to place scallops in heated skillet and cook 5 to 8 minutes or until lightly browned, turning once. Place scallops on a serving dish, cover, and keep warm until ready to serve.

In a small bowl, combine cornstarch and water; stir until smooth. Pour reserved lemon juice mixture into a small saucepan. Bring to a boil. Stirring constantly, add cornstarch mixture. Bring to a boil and cook 5 to 8 minutes or until thickened. Serve with scallops.
Yield: about 5 dozen appetizers

1 serving (1 ounce or 2 to 3 scallops): 71 calories, 1.4 gms fat, 9.4 gms protein, 5.0 gms carbohydrate

For a taste-tempting treat, tender scallops are wrapped in thin slices of prosciutto and dipped in a warm, tangy sauce. Scrumptious Stuffed Potatoes feature a flavorful mushroom and onion filling topped with cheese and chives.

STUFFED POTATOES

10 small russet potatoes, baked
 2 cups fat-free cottage cheese
 1 teaspoon salt
¼ teaspoon ground black pepper
 2 tablespoons reduced-calorie
       margarine
 1 cup finely chopped onions
 1 cup chopped fresh mushrooms
 1 clove garlic, minced
   Vegetable cooking spray
 2 cups (8 ounces) finely shredded
       fat-free Cheddar cheese
¼ cup chopped fresh chives

Preheat oven to 375 degrees. Cut potatoes in half lengthwise. Leaving about ½ inch of pulp on skins, scoop out remaining pulp and place in a large bowl. Add cottage cheese, salt, and pepper to potato pulp; stir until well blended and set aside.

In a medium skillet, melt margarine over medium heat. Add onions, mushrooms, and garlic; cook until onions are tender. Add onion mixture to potato mixture; stir until well blended. Spoon mixture into potato skins and place on a baking sheet sprayed with cooking spray. Sprinkle cheese and chives evenly over stuffed potatoes. Bake 8 to 10 minutes or until cheese is bubbly. Serve warm.
Yield: 20 stuffed potato halves

1 serving (½ potato): 96 calories, 0.7 gms fat, 7.1 gms protein, 15.2 gms carbohydrate

BREADED VEGETABLES WITH MARINARA SAUCE

SAUCE

Olive oil cooking spray
1 cup finely chopped sweet red pepper
½ cup finely chopped onion
1 clove garlic, minced
1 can (29 ounces) tomato sauce
1 can (14½ ounces) Italian-style stewed tomatoes, undrained
1 teaspoon dried parsley flakes
1 teaspoon granulated sugar
½ teaspoon dried oregano leaves
½ teaspoon dried basil leaves
½ teaspoon dried thyme leaves
½ teaspoon salt
¼ teaspoon ground black pepper

Shredded Parmesan cheese for garnish

BREADED VEGETABLES

1½ cups finely crushed corn flake cereal
½ cup grated Parmesan cheese
1 teaspoon paprika
½ teaspoon salt
4 egg whites, beaten
4 large carrots, cut into ½ x 3-inch sticks
2 medium zucchini, cut into ½ x 3-inch sticks
8 ounces whole fresh mushrooms
Olive oil cooking spray

For sauce, spray a large saucepan with cooking spray. Combine red pepper, onion, and garlic in saucepan. Cook over medium heat until onion is tender. Add remaining ingredients; stir until well blended. Bring to a boil, reduce heat to low, cover, and simmer 30 minutes. Cover and keep warm until ready to serve.

For breaded vegetables, preheat oven to 375 degrees. In a medium bowl, combine cereal, cheese, paprika, and salt. Place egg whites in a shallow bowl. Dip vegetables, one at a time, in egg whites. Coat with cereal mixture. Place on a baking sheet sprayed with cooking spray. Bake 20 to 25 minutes or until golden brown. Transfer sauce to a serving bowl and garnish with shredded cheese. Serve vegetables with sauce.

Yield: about 8 dozen pieces of vegetable and 5½ cups sauce or 20 servings

1 serving (5 pieces of vegetable and ¼ cup sauce): 61 calories, 1.0 gms fat, 3.6 gms protein, 10.7 gms carbohydrate

Breaded Vegetables to serve with Marinara Sauce are baked instead of fried for a healthier snack. Horseradish Beef Rolls are easy to make by placing thin slices of roast beef and a creamy spread inside a fluffy biscuit wrapper.

HORSERADISH BEEF ROLLS

½ cup fat-free cottage cheese
2 tablespoons prepared horseradish
2 teaspoons Dijon-style mustard
1 pound thinly sliced lean cooked roast beef, trimmed of fat
2 cans (10 biscuits each) refrigerated buttermilk biscuits
Vegetable cooking spray

Preheat oven to 450 degrees. For sauce, combine cottage cheese, horseradish, and mustard in a blender or food processor; process until smooth. Cut or fold each slice of roast beef into a 3-inch square. On a lightly floured surface, use a floured rolling pin to roll each biscuit into a 4-inch square. Spread a heaping teaspoonful of sauce over biscuit. Place two 3-inch squares roast beef over sauce. Roll up biscuit and place, seam side down, on a baking sheet sprayed with cooking spray. Bake 8 to 10 minutes or until golden brown. Serve warm with remaining sauce.

Yield: 20 beef rolls

1 serving (1 beef roll): 105 calories, 3.2 gms fat, 8.9 gms protein, 10.5 gms carbohydrate

Maraschino cherries frozen in ice cubes add a festive look to our fruity Christmas Tea. Featuring layers of angel food cake and reduced-fat ice cream, Praline Ice Cream Cake is proof that a low-calorie dessert can be delicious, too! Light and crispy, Cinnamon Popcorn Snack Mix is sure to be a crowd-pleaser.

CHRISTMAS TEA

Maraschino cherries with stems, drained and frozen in ice cubes
2 quarts water, divided
3 large tea bags
1 can (6 ounces) frozen orange juice concentrate, thawed
2 teaspoons orange extract
12 packets sugar substitute

In a large saucepan or Dutch oven, bring 1 quart water to a boil. Remove from heat. Add tea bags; let stand 15 minutes. Remove tea bags. Stir in remaining 1 quart cold water. Add remaining ingredients; stir until well blended. Cover and refrigerate until well chilled. To serve, pour tea over prepared ice cubes.
Yield: about ten 6-ounce servings

1 serving (6 ounces tea): 32 calories, 0.1 gms fat, 0.5 gms protein, 8.3 gms carbohydrate

CINNAMON POPCORN SNACK MIX

10 cups popped popcorn, cooked without salt or fat
2 egg whites
1 cup granulated sugar
1 teaspoon ground cinnamon
1 teaspoon salt

Preheat oven to 225 degrees. Place popcorn in a large bowl. In a small bowl, beat egg whites until stiff. Beat in sugar, cinnamon, and salt. Spoon egg white mixture over popcorn; stir until well coated. Spread evenly on a greased baking sheet. Bake 1 hour, stirring every 15 minutes. Cool completely on pan. Store in an airtight container.
Yield: about 8 cups snack mix

1 serving (1 cup snack mix): 126 calories, 0 gms fat, 2.1 gms protein, 30.3 gms carbohydrate

PRALINE ICE CREAM CAKE

1 angel food cake
4 cups reduced-fat praline and caramel ice cream, softened
1 container (12½ ounces) caramel ice cream topping, divided

Cut cake horizontally into thirds. Spread about 2 cups ice cream between each layer of cake. Drizzle about ¼ cup topping over top of cake. Cover and freeze until firm. To serve, cut into slices and drizzle with remaining topping.
Yield: about 16 servings

1 serving (¹⁄₁₆ of recipe): 217 calories, 1.4 gms fat, 5.9 gms protein, 46.2 gms carbohydrate

ORANGE CHEESECAKES

12 vanilla wafers
1½ cups (12 ounces) fat-free cream cheese, softened
1 cup fat-free sour cream
½ cup granulated sugar
½ cup frozen egg substitute, thawed
2 tablespoons all-purpose flour
2 teaspoons orange extract
1 can (11 ounces) mandarin oranges, well drained
⅛ cup orange marmalade

Preheat oven to 350 degrees. Place 1 vanilla wafer into bottom of each tin of a paper-lined muffin pan. In a medium bowl, beat cream cheese until fluffy. Add sour cream, sugar, egg substitute, flour, and orange extract; beat until smooth. Spoon cheese mixture over vanilla wafers, filling each tin full. Bake 18 minutes. Turn oven off and leave in oven 2 minutes. Leaving oven door ajar, leave in oven 15 minutes longer. Cool completely in pan.

In a small bowl, combine oranges and marmalade. Spoon orange mixture on top of each cheesecake. Loosely cover and store in refrigerator. Serve chilled.
Yield: 1 dozen cheesecakes

1 serving (1 cheesecake): 110 calories, 0.6 gms fat, 6.6 gms protein, 18.2 gms carbohydrate

PRALINE COFFEE

2 quarts brewed coffee
3 cans (12 ounces each) evaporated skim milk
½ cup firmly packed brown sugar
3 cups fat-free vanilla ice cream, softened
1 cup vodka
1 tablespoon vanilla extract
2 teaspoons maple flavoring

In a Dutch oven, combine coffee, milk, and sugar. Stirring occasionally, cook over medium-high heat until mixture begins to boil; remove from heat. Stir in ice cream, vodka, vanilla, and maple flavoring. Serve hot.
Yield: about twenty 6-ounce servings

1 serving (6 ounces coffee): 113 calories, 0.1 gms fat, 5.1 gms protein, 16.2 gms carbohydrate, 3.7 gms alcohol

Fat-free vanilla ice cream and vodka lend holiday appeal to luscious Praline Coffee, and Sinless Brownies are moist, chewy treats. Mandarin oranges and marmalade add a colorful touch to miniature low-fat Orange Cheesecakes.

SINLESS BROWNIES

1½ cups granulated sugar
1 cup all-purpose flour
⅓ cup cocoa
½ teaspoon baking powder
¼ teaspoon salt
¼ cup frozen egg substitute, thawed
¼ cup water
1 egg white
2 tablespoons reduced-calorie margarine, softened
1 tablespoon vanilla extract
Vegetable cooking spray

Preheat oven to 350 degrees. In a medium bowl, combine sugar, flour, cocoa, baking powder, and salt. Add egg substitute, water, egg white, margarine, and vanilla; stir until well blended. Spoon batter into an 8-inch square baking pan sprayed with cooking spray. Bake 25 to 30 minutes or until dry on top and set in center. Cut into 2-inch squares.
Yield: about 16 brownies

1 serving (one 2-inch square brownie): 97 calories, 1.0 gms fat, 1.5 gms protein, 22.3 gms carbohydrate

RISE AND SHINE BREAKFAST

When Christmas finally arrives after weeks of busy preparations, it's nice to be able to relax and enjoy the celebration. This delightful breakfast will make sure the day gets off to a perfect start. The quick recipes here can all be prepared ahead of time and then refrigerated. When mealtime arrives, the dishes that aren't served chilled are simply popped in the oven — so you can spend Christmas morning around the tree with family and friends, instead of in the kitchen!

Featuring a savory cheese grits crust and a hearty filling of eggs, Cheddar cheese, sausage, and green onions, Sausage-Grits Pie makes a delicious main dish.

SAUSAGE-GRITS PIE

CRUST
- 1½ cups water
- ½ teaspoon garlic powder
- ½ cup quick-cooking grits
- ½ cup (2 ounces) shredded Cheddar cheese
- ¼ cup all-purpose flour
- 1 egg, beaten

FILLING
- 6 eggs
- ½ teaspoon dry mustard
- ½ teaspoon salt
- ¼ teaspoon ground black pepper
- ½ pound ground mild pork sausage, cooked, drained, and crumbled
- 1 cup (4 ounces) shredded Cheddar cheese
- 4 green onions, chopped

For crust, combine water and garlic powder in a medium saucepan. Bring to a boil. Stir in grits and bring to a boil again. Reduce heat to medium-low, cover, and cook 5 to 7 minutes or until thick, stirring occasionally. Remove from heat. In a small bowl, combine cheese, flour, and egg. Stir cheese mixture into grits. Press grits mixture into bottom and 2 inches up sides of a greased 9-inch springform pan.

Preheat oven to 350 degrees. For filling, whisk eggs, mustard, salt, and pepper in a large bowl. Stir in sausage, cheese, and onions. Pour into crust. Bake 45 to 50 minutes or until a knife inserted in center comes out clean. Serve hot or cool completely on a wire rack, cover, and refrigerate until ready to reheat.

To reheat, cover and bake in a preheated 350-degree oven 30 to 35 minutes or until heated through. Remove sides of pan. Serve warm.
Yield: 8 to 10 servings

Flavored with cinnamon, nutmeg, and orange liqueur, Oven-Baked French Toast is sprinkled with raisins and pecans for a delightful treat. Warm syrup with a hint of orange makes a yummy topping.

OVEN-BAKED FRENCH TOAST

- 8 ½-inch-thick slices French bread (about one-half of a 1-pound loaf)
- ½ cup raisins
- ½ cup chopped pecans
- 6 eggs
- 2 cups half and half
- ½ cup orange-flavored liqueur
- 1 teaspoon ground cinnamon
- ½ teaspoon salt
- ¼ teaspoon ground nutmeg

  Sifted confectioners sugar or Orange Syrup (recipe this page) to serve

Arrange bread slices in a single layer, with sides touching, in a greased jellyroll pan. Sprinkle raisins and pecans over bread. In a medium bowl, whisk eggs, half and half, liqueur, cinnamon, salt, and nutmeg. Pour egg mixture over bread. Cover and refrigerate 8 hours or overnight.

Preheat oven to 400 degrees. Uncover and bake French toast 30 to 35 minutes or until a toothpick inserted in center comes out clean and toast is light brown. To serve, dust with confectioners sugar or pour Orange Syrup over slices of toast.
Yield: 8 servings

ORANGE SYRUP

- 1 bottle (12 ounces) pancake syrup
- 1 teaspoon orange extract

In a small saucepan, heat syrup until hot. Remove from heat; stir in orange extract. Serve with French toast.
Yield: about 1½ cups syrup

A creamy chocolate-peanut butter filling is hidden in the center of these taste-tempting oat bran Surprise Muffins (*left*). Delectable pinwheel Praline Biscuits feature a luscious swirl of chopped pecans and brown sugar.

PRALINE BISCUITS

- 1 cup chopped pecans
- ¼ cup firmly packed brown sugar
- 3 tablespoons butter or margarine, melted
- 1 teaspoon maple extract
- 2 cups all-purpose flour
- 2 teaspoons granulated sugar
- 1 teaspoon baking powder
- ½ teaspoon baking soda
- ¼ teaspoon salt
- ½ cup vegetable shortening
- ¾ cup milk

In a small bowl, combine pecans, brown sugar, butter, and maple extract; set aside.

In a medium bowl, combine flour, granulated sugar, baking powder, baking soda, and salt. Using a pastry blender or 2 knives, cut in shortening until mixture resembles coarse meal. Add milk, stirring just until moistened. Turn dough onto a lightly floured surface and knead about 2 minutes. Use a floured rolling pin to roll dough into an 8 x 12-inch rectangle; spread pecan mixture over dough. Starting with 1 long side, roll up jelly-roll fashion. Using a serrated knife, cut into twelve 1-inch-thick slices. Place slices, with sides touching, in a greased 7 x 11-inch baking dish. Cover and refrigerate until ready to bake.

Preheat oven to 400 degrees. Uncover biscuits and bake 22 to 25 minutes or until light brown. Serve warm.
Yield: 1 dozen biscuits

SURPRISE MUFFINS

- ½ cup smooth peanut butter
- ½ cup semisweet chocolate chips
- 1½ cups all-purpose flour
- 1 cup oat bran
- ½ cup firmly packed brown sugar
- 2½ teaspoons baking powder
- ¼ teaspoon salt
- 1 cup milk
- ⅓ cup vegetable oil
- 2 eggs
- 1 teaspoon maple extract

Preheat oven to 425 degrees. In a small bowl, combine peanut butter and chocolate chips; set aside.

In a medium bowl, combine flour, bran, sugar, baking powder, and salt. In a small bowl, whisk milk, oil, eggs, and maple extract. Make a well in center of dry ingredients and add milk mixture. Stir just until moistened. Spoon about 2 tablespoons batter into each tin of a greased muffin pan. Spoon about 2 teaspoons peanut butter mixture over batter in each tin. Spoon remaining batter over peanut butter mixture, filling each tin ¾ full. Bake 15 to 18 minutes or until muffins pull away from sides of pan. Remove from pan and cool completely on a wire rack. Store in an airtight container. Muffins may be served at room temperature or reheated. To reheat, cover and bake in a preheated 350-degree oven 5 to 8 minutes or until heated through.
Yield: about 1 dozen muffins

MUSHROOM PIE

CRUST
- 1½ cups all-purpose flour
- ½ teaspoon salt
- ½ cup vegetable shortening
- ¼ cup cold water

FILLING
- ½ cup butter or margarine
- ½ cup chopped green onions
- 3 cloves garlic, minced
- 10 ounces fresh mushrooms, sliced
- 2 cups shredded Swiss cheese
- 3 eggs
- 1⅓ cups whipping cream
- 1 teaspoon dried basil leaves, crushed
- 1 teaspoon dried thyme leaves, crushed
- 1 teaspoon salt
- ½ teaspoon ground black pepper

For crust, preheat oven to 450 degrees. In a medium bowl, combine flour and salt. Using a pastry blender or 2 knives, cut in shortening until mixture resembles coarse meal. Sprinkle with water; mix until a soft dough forms. On a lightly floured surface, use a floured rolling pin to roll out dough to ⅛-inch thickness. Transfer to an ungreased 9-inch deep-dish pie plate and use a sharp knife to trim edge of dough. Prick bottom of crust with a fork. Bake 5 minutes. Cool completely on a wire rack. Reduce oven temperature to 375 degrees.

For filling, melt butter in a large skillet over medium heat. Add onions and garlic; cook until onions are tender. Add mushrooms; cook until all liquid has evaporated. Remove from heat. Sprinkle half of cheese over crust. Spoon half of mushroom mixture over cheese. Repeat with remaining cheese and mushroom mixture.

In a medium bowl, whisk eggs, cream, basil, thyme, salt, and pepper. Pour egg mixture into pie crust. Bake 40 to 45 minutes or until a knife inserted in center of pie comes out clean. Let stand 10 minutes before serving. Serve warm.

Pie may be made in advance. Cool slightly, cover, and refrigerate. To reheat, cover and bake in a preheated 350-degree oven 40 to 45 minutes or until heated through.
Yield: 8 to 10 servings

Seasoned with garlic, basil, and thyme and loaded with Swiss cheese, Mushroom Pie makes a flavorful addition to your Christmas morning meal. Refreshingly different Minty Fruit Salad is tossed with a sweet mixture of honey and maraschino cherry juice.

MINTY FRUIT SALAD

- 1 jar (10 ounces) whole maraschino cherries
- 6 oranges, peeled and chopped
- 3 bananas, peeled and sliced
- ½ cup pomegranate seeds
- ¼ cup chopped fresh mint leaves
- 2 tablespoons honey

Fresh mint leaves for garnish

Drain cherries, reserving juice. In a large bowl, combine cherries, oranges, bananas, pomegranate seeds, and chopped mint. In a small bowl, combine reserved cherry juice and honey. Pour honey mixture over fruit; stir until well coated. Garnish with mint leaves. Serve chilled.
Yield: about six 1-cup servings

Cool and creamy, Pineapple Frost is the perfect beverage to serve with breakfast. Overnight Coffee Cake *(top)* is a tasty, simple-to-fix treat. A pleasing combination of spinach, eggs, and cheeses baked atop croissant halves, Spinach-Feta Strata is sure to be a hit with holiday company.

SPINACH-FETA STRATA

    6 croissants, cut in half horizontally
    6 eggs, beaten
1½ cups milk
    1 package (10 ounces) frozen
         chopped spinach, thawed and
         well drained
 ½ teaspoon salt
 ¼ teaspoon ground black pepper
 ¼ teaspoon ground nutmeg
1½ cups (6 ounces) shredded Monterey
         Jack cheese
    7 ounces crumbled feta cheese

Arrange croissant halves with sides overlapping in a greased 9 x 13-inch baking dish. In a medium bowl, combine eggs, milk, spinach, salt, pepper, and nutmeg. Pour over croissants. Sprinkle cheeses over spinach mixture. Cover and refrigerate 8 hours or overnight.

Preheat oven to 350 degrees. Uncover and bake 40 to 45 minutes or until light brown. Cut into squares. Serve warm.
Yield: about 15 servings

OVERNIGHT COFFEE CAKE

    1 cup chopped pecans
 ¾ cup firmly packed brown sugar
    1 box (4 ounces) instant vanilla
         pudding and pie filling mix
    1 teaspoon ground cinnamon
    1 package (2½ ounces) frozen white
         dinner rolls, thawed according to
         package directions
 ¾ cup butter or margarine, melted

In a small bowl, combine pecans, sugar, pudding mix, and cinnamon. Sprinkle 3 tablespoons sugar mixture in bottom of a greased 10-inch tube pan. Dip each roll in butter and place in sugar mixture in bowl; spoon sugar mixture over, covering each roll completely. Place rolls in pan in a single layer with sides touching. Sprinkle remaining sugar mixture over rolls. Pour remaining butter over rolls. Cover and refrigerate 8 hours or overnight.

Remove pan from refrigerator 30 minutes before baking, leave covered, and place in a warm place (80 to 85 degrees) to allow rolls to rise. Preheat oven to 350 degrees. Uncover and bake 40 to 45 minutes or until golden brown. Cover with foil if top browns too quickly. Cool in pan 15 minutes. Remove from pan and serve warm.
Yield: about 16 servings

PINEAPPLE FROST

- 3 cups pineapple sherbet, softened
- 2 cans (8 ounces each) crushed pineapple, drained
- 2 cups half and half
- ⅔ cup light corn syrup
- 1 quart ginger ale, chilled

In a blender or food processor, process sherbet, pineapple, half and half, and corn syrup until pineapple is very finely chopped. Pour into a medium bowl, cover, and freeze until firm.

One hour before serving, remove from freezer. To serve, place pineapple mixture in a 3-quart container, pour ginger ale over, and stir to make a slush.
Yield: about thirteen 6-ounce servings

CRANBERRY-BLUE CHEESE SALAD

- 2 cans (8 ounces each) pineapple tidbits, undrained
- 1 can (16 ounces) whole berry cranberry sauce
- 1 box (6 ounces) raspberry-flavored gelatin
- ⅓ cup plus 2 tablespoons cream sherry, divided
- 3 ounces blue cheese, crumbled and divided
- ½ very ripe banana, mashed
- 1 teaspoon lemon juice
- ½ cup whipping cream
- 2 ounces cream cheese, softened

  Orange peel for garnish

Place a small bowl and beaters from an electric mixer in freezer until well chilled. Place pineapple and cranberry sauce in a medium saucepan; bring to a boil. Remove from heat; add gelatin and stir until gelatin dissolves. Cool 5 minutes. Stir in ⅓ cup sherry and 2 ounces blue cheese. Pour into a 6-cup mold, cover, and refrigerate until firm.

In a small bowl, combine banana and lemon juice. In chilled bowl, beat cream and cream cheese until stiff peaks form. Beat in remaining 2 tablespoons sherry and 1 ounce blue cheese. Beat in banana mixture. Cover and refrigerate until ready to serve.

To serve, dip bottom of mold into hot water; invert onto a serving plate. Spoon banana mixture over gelatin. Garnish with orange peel.
Yield: about 12 servings

A colorful side dish chock-full of pineapple tidbits, Cranberry-Blue Cheese Salad features an unusual blend of flavors. Crunchy granola, mellow fruit, and a mixture of cream cheese and yogurt are layered to create these wonderful, low-fat Granola-Fruit Parfaits.

GRANOLA-FRUIT PARFAITS

- 2 cups low-fat granola cereal
- 4 kiwifruit, peeled and cut into pieces
- 1 can (20 ounces) pineapple chunks, well drained
- 1 container (8 ounces) fat-free cream cheese, softened
- 1 cup fat-free vanilla-flavored yogurt

Spoon half of granola into 6 parfait glasses. Arrange half of kiwifruit and pineapple over granola. Repeat layers with remaining granola and fruit.

In a small bowl, beat cream cheese and yogurt until smooth. Cover cream cheese mixture and parfaits and refrigerate until ready to serve.

To serve, spoon cream cheese mixture over parfaits.
Yield: 6 servings

A nutty vanilla wafer crust and a sweet custard filling are topped with fresh kiwi slices to make this colorful Kiwi Tart. A delicate apple jelly glaze is brushed over the fruit for a flavorful finishing touch.

KIWI TART

CRUST
    2 cups finely crushed vanilla wafer
        cookies (about 48 cookies)
    ½ cup finely ground pecans
    ½ cup butter or margarine, melted

FILLING
    1 cup milk
    1 cup whipping cream
    1 package (8 ounces) cream cheese,
        softened
    1 vanilla bean, cut in half lengthwise
    6 egg yolks
    1 cup granulated sugar
    2 tablespoons all-purpose flour
    6 kiwifruit, peeled and cut into
        ⅛-inch slices

GLAZE
    1 teaspoon cornstarch
    1 teaspoon water
    3 tablespoons apple jelly

For crust, preheat oven to 350 degrees. In a medium bowl, combine cookie crumbs, pecans, and butter. Press into bottom and up sides of an 11-inch tart pan with removable bottom. Bake 12 to 15 minutes or until light brown. Cool completely on a wire rack. Remove crust from pan and place on a serving plate.

For filling, combine milk, cream, cream cheese, and vanilla bean in a large saucepan. Stirring constantly, bring to a boil over medium heat; remove from heat. Cover and let stand 15 minutes. Remove vanilla bean and use a sharp knife to scrape black seeds from bean into milk mixture. Return bean to milk mixture.

In a small bowl, whisk egg yolks, sugar, and flour. Add about ½ cup milk mixture to egg mixture; stir until well blended. Add egg mixture to milk mixture in saucepan. Stirring constantly, bring to a boil over medium heat and cook 2 minutes or until thickened. Remove vanilla bean. Pour filling into crust. Cover and refrigerate until well chilled. Arrange kiwifruit over filling.

For glaze, combine cornstarch and water in a small bowl; stir until smooth. In a small saucepan, melt jelly over medium heat. Whisk cornstarch mixture into jelly and cook until slightly thickened. Brush glaze evenly over kiwifruit. Loosely cover and store in refrigerator.
Yield: 8 to 10 servings

HAZELNUT TORTE

TORTE
    2½ cups whole unsalted hazelnuts
    4   eggs
    ¾   cup granulated sugar
    ½   cup butter or margarine, melted
    ⅓   cup light corn syrup
    ¼   cup milk
    2   teaspoons vanilla extract
    1¼ cups all-purpose flour
    1   teaspoon baking powder
    ½   teaspoon salt
    ¼   teaspoon baking soda
    ¼   teaspoon ground cinnamon

FILLING
    1 box (3 ounces) vanilla pudding and
        pie filling mix
    1½ cups milk
    ½   cup amaretto

BUTTERCREAM FROSTING
    4 cups sifted confectioners sugar
    1 cup butter or margarine, softened
    3 tablespoons milk
    1 teaspoon vanilla extract

A wreath of holly created with frosting and candies adds a festive look to this Hazelnut Torte. The dessert is made by spooning a delicious vanilla pudding filling enhanced with amaretto between thin layers of delicate, nutty cake. Buttercream frosting completes the tempting treat.

DECORATIVE FROSTING

- ⅓ cup water
- 2 tablespoons meringue powder
- 6 cups sifted confectioners sugar, divided
- 1¼ cups vegetable shortening
- 1 teaspoon vanilla extract
  Green paste food coloring
  Red cinnamon candies

For torte, preheat oven to 350 degrees. Spread hazelnuts on an ungreased baking sheet. Bake 8 to 10 minutes or until nuts are slightly darker in color. Cool completely on pan. In a blender or food processor, process hazelnuts until finely ground; set aside.

In a large bowl, beat eggs at medium speed of an electric mixer 5 minutes. Continue beating 5 minutes longer while adding sugar 1 tablespoon at a time. Beat in butter, corn syrup, milk, and vanilla. In a medium bowl, sift next 5 ingredients. Add dry ingredients to egg mixture; beat at low speed until moistened. Stir in hazelnuts. Pour batter into 2 greased and floured 9-inch round cake pans. Bake 25 to 30 minutes or until cake begins to pull away from sides of pan and top springs back when lightly pressed. Cool in pans 15 minutes; remove from pans. Cool on a wire rack. Slice each layer in half horizontally. Separate layers with waxed paper; cover and freeze until firm.

For filling, combine pudding mix and milk in a medium saucepan. Stirring constantly, cook over medium heat until mixture comes to a rolling boil. Stir in amaretto and bring to a boil again. Cover and refrigerate until well chilled. Spread filling evenly between cake layers.

For buttercream frosting, combine all ingredients in a large bowl; beat until smooth. Frost sides and top of cake. Transfer remaining frosting to a pastry bag fitted with a small star tip. Pipe a decorative border along bottom edge of cake.

For decorative frosting, combine water and meringue powder in a medium bowl; beat until soft peaks form. Add 2 cups sugar, beating until well blended. Alternately add shortening and remaining 4 cups sugar; beat until well blended. Beat in vanilla. Tint frosting green. Transfer frosting to a pastry bag fitted with a large leaf tip (we used tip #112). Pipe leaves on top of cake for wreath design. Place candies on leaves. Cover and store in refrigerator.

Yield: about 20 servings

147

Banana Split Dessert (*left*) is a delectable combination of bananas, ice cream, chocolate sauce, whipped cream, pecans, and maraschino cherries. Smooth and rich Almond Cappuccino is the perfect accompaniment to dessert. Cherry Cobbler Pie features a mouth-watering cream cheese filling and a delightful cinnamon crumb topping.

BANANA SPLIT DESSERT

CRUST
- 1½ cups graham cracker crumbs
- 2 tablespoons granulated sugar
- 5 tablespoons butter or margarine, melted

FILLING
- 5 bananas, peeled and cut into ¼-inch slices
- ½ gallon cookies and cream ice cream, softened

SAUCE
- 1 can (12 ounces) evaporated milk
- 1 package (6 ounces) semisweet chocolate chips
- ½ cup butter or margarine
- 2 cups sifted confectioners sugar

TOPPING
- 2 cups whipping cream
- ½ cup granulated sugar
- 1 cup chopped pecans
- 1 jar (6 ounces) maraschino cherries, drained and chopped

For crust, combine cracker crumbs and sugar in a small bowl. Add butter; stir until crumbly. Press crumb mixture into bottom of a greased 9 x 13-inch baking dish.

For filling, arrange banana slices over crust. Spread ice cream over bananas. Cover and freeze until firm.

For sauce, combine milk, chocolate chips, and butter in a medium saucepan. Stirring constantly, cook over low heat until smooth. Increase heat to medium. Gradually stir in sugar and bring to a boil. Stirring constantly, reduce heat to medium-low and boil 8 minutes. Remove from heat; cool to room temperature. Spread sauce over ice cream and return to freezer.

For topping, place a large bowl and beaters from an electric mixer in refrigerator until well chilled. In chilled bowl, whip cream until soft peaks form. Gradually add sugar; whip until stiff peaks form. Spread whipped cream evenly over fudge sauce. Sprinkle pecans and cherries evenly over whipped cream. Cover and store in freezer until ready to serve. To serve, remove from freezer 15 to 20 minutes before serving. Cut into about 2-inch squares.
Yield: about 24 servings

ALMOND CAPPUCCINO

- 2 quarts brewed coffee
- 1 quart evaporated skim milk
- ½ cup firmly packed brown sugar
- 1 tablespoon vanilla extract
- 1 teaspoon almond extract

In a large saucepan or Dutch oven, combine coffee, milk, and sugar. Stirring occasionally, cook over medium-high heat until mixture begins to boil; remove from heat. Stir in extracts. Serve hot.
Yield: about sixteen 6-ounce servings

CHOCOLATE-ORANGE CHEESECAKES

CHOCOLATE MINT LEAVES
- ¼ cup semisweet chocolate chips
- 1 tablespoon butter or margarine
- 3 dozen fresh mint leaves, washed and patted dry

CHEESECAKES
- 6 large oranges (do not use navel oranges)
- 1 envelope unflavored gelatin
- ¼ cup hot water
- 2 packages (8 ounces each) cream cheese, softened
- 2 cups sifted confectioners sugar
- ½ cup orange-flavored liqueur
- 1 teaspoon orange extract
- 1 package (6 ounces) semisweet chocolate chips, melted

TOPPING
- 1 package (3 ounces) cream cheese, softened
- 1 cup sifted confectioners sugar
- 1 teaspoon orange extract
- 1 cup whipping cream

For chocolate leaves, melt chocolate chips and butter in a small saucepan over low heat, stirring constantly. Use a small paintbrush to brush chocolate mixture onto tops of leaves. Transfer to waxed paper. Allow chocolate to harden in a cool, dry place.

For cheesecakes, cut oranges in half crosswise. Cut a thin slice off bottom of each orange half so orange half will sit flat. Leaving flesh and shells intact, use a small paring knife to remove flesh from orange halves; set aside.

In a small bowl, dissolve gelatin in water. In a large bowl, beat cream cheese and sugar until fluffy. Add gelatin mixture, liqueur, and orange extract; beat until well blended. Gradually beat in chocolate chips. Spoon chocolate mixture into each orange shell. Cover and refrigerate until firm.

For topping, place a large bowl and beaters from an electric mixer in freezer until well chilled. In a medium bowl, beat cream cheese, sugar, and orange extract until fluffy. In chilled bowl, whip cream until stiff peaks form; beat in cream cheese mixture.

For each cheesecake, separate sections from 1 orange half; arrange on top of cheesecake. Spoon a heaping tablespoonful topping over each orange half. Garnish with chocolate leaves. Cover loosely with plastic wrap and refrigerate until ready to serve.
Yield: 12 servings

These Chocolate-Orange Cheesecakes are unique treats! Orange flavoring enhances the chocolate cheesecake, which is served in orange shells topped with fresh fruit, whipped topping, and chocolate-coated mint leaves.

CHERRY COBBLER PIE

CRUST
- 2 cups graham cracker crumbs
- ½ cup all-purpose flour
- ½ cup butter or margarine, melted
- ¼ cup granulated sugar

FILLING
- 1 package (8 ounces) cream cheese, softened
- ½ cup granulated sugar
- ¼ cup cherry-flavored liqueur
- 1 tablespoon all-purpose flour
- 1 teaspoon dried grated lemon peel
- 2 cans (16 ounces each) tart red pitted cherries, undrained
- ¼ cup cornstarch
- 1 cup granulated sugar

TOPPING
- ⅓ cup all-purpose flour
- 2 tablespoons granulated sugar
- 2 tablespoons butter or margarine, melted
- ½ teaspoon vanilla extract
- ⅛ teaspoon ground cinnamon

For crust, combine all ingredients in a medium bowl until well blended. Press into bottom and 2 inches up sides of a greased 10-inch springform pan; set aside.

For filling, beat cream cheese, sugar, liqueur, flour, and lemon peel in a medium bowl until well blended. Spread cream cheese mixture over crust.

Reserving ¼ cup juice, drain cherries. In a small bowl, combine cornstarch and reserved cherry juice; stir until smooth. In a medium saucepan, combine cherries and sugar. Stirring occasionally, cook over medium heat until sugar dissolves and mixture comes to a boil. Stirring constantly, add cornstarch mixture and cook until thickened. Pour over cream cheese mixture.

Preheat oven to 350 degrees. For topping, combine all ingredients in a small bowl. Sprinkle topping around edge of filling. Bake 30 minutes. Preheat broiler and broil 2 minutes or until topping is golden brown. Cool completely on a wire rack. Remove sides of pan and refrigerate until well chilled.
Yield: about 16 servings

BLUEBERRIES AND CREAM CHEESECAKE

CRUST
- 1 package (12 ounces) vanilla wafer cookies, finely crushed
- ¾ cup butter or margarine, melted

FILLING
- 5 packages (8 ounces each) cream cheese, softened
- 1½ cups granulated sugar
- 6 eggs
- 2 egg yolks
- 3 tablespoons all-purpose flour
- 3 teaspoons vanilla extract
- ¼ cup whipping cream

TOPPING
- 3 tablespoons cornstarch
- 1 cup plus 3 tablespoons water, divided
- 1 cup granulated sugar
- 1 package (16 ounces) frozen unsweetened blueberries, thawed and drained

For crust, combine cookie crumbs and butter. Press into bottom and halfway up sides of a greased 9-inch springform pan. Cover and refrigerate.

For filling, beat cream cheese 25 minutes in a large bowl, adding 1 package at a time. Add sugar and beat 5 minutes longer. Add eggs and egg yolks, one at a time, beating 2 minutes after each addition. Beat in flour and vanilla. Beat in cream. Preheat oven to 500 degrees. Pour filling into crust. Bake 10 minutes. Reduce heat to 200 degrees. Bake 1 hour. Turn oven off and leave cake in oven 1 hour without opening door. Cool completely on a wire rack. Remove sides of pan.

For topping, combine cornstarch and 3 tablespoons water in a small bowl; stir until smooth. Combine sugar and remaining 1 cup water in a small saucepan. Stirring constantly, cook over medium heat until sugar dissolves. Stirring constantly, add cornstarch mixture and cook until mixture boils and thickens. Remove from heat and cool to room temperature. Stir in blueberries. Spoon topping over cheesecake. Loosely cover and refrigerate 8 hours or overnight. Serve chilled.

Yield: about 16 servings

Luscious dark berries gleam like polished gemstones atop this moist Blueberries and Cream Cheesecake. A pleasing blend of Burgundy, brandy, and cranberry juice, Cranberry Sangria is garnished with colorful fruit kabobs.

Your guests will find this beautifully decorated Chocolate-Mocha Cake irresistible! Loaded with chocolate chips, the devil's food cake is enhanced by coffee and coffee-flavored liqueur.

CRANBERRY SANGRIA

- 1 bottle (750 ml) Burgundy
- 3 cups cranberry juice
- ¼ cup brandy
- ¼ cup granulated sugar
- 1 can (8 ounces) pineapple chunks, drained
- 1 orange, thinly sliced
  Maraschino cherries
  Wooden skewers

Combine Burgundy, cranberry juice, brandy, and sugar in a 2-quart container. Stir until sugar dissolves. Cover and refrigerate until ready to serve.

Place pieces of fruit on wooden skewers; place in glasses. Add ice and pour sangria into glasses.

Yield: about eight 6-ounce servings

CHOCOLATE-MOCHA CAKE

CAKE

- 1 box (18.25 ounces) devil's food cake mix
- 3 eggs
- 1 cup coffee-flavored liqueur
- ½ cup vegetable oil
- ⅓ cup brewed coffee
- 1 cup semisweet chocolate chips

FROSTING

- 5¼ cups sifted confectioners sugar
- 1½ cups butter or margarine, softened
- 3 tablespoons milk
- 1 teaspoon vanilla extract

  Gold cord, garlands, ribbon, and jewel stones to decorate

For cake, preheat oven to 350 degrees. In a large bowl, combine cake mix, eggs, liqueur, oil, and coffee. Mix according to cake mix instructions. Stir in chocolate

chips. Pour batter into a greased and floured 9 x 13-inch baking pan. Bake 35 to 40 minutes or until cake begins to pull away from sides of pan and top springs back when lightly pressed. Cool in pan 10 minutes. Remove from pan and cool completely on a wire rack.

For frosting, combine all ingredients in a medium bowl; beat until smooth. Reserving 1 cup frosting, frost sides and top of cake. Transfer remaining frosting to a pastry bag fitted with a large star tip. Pipe decorative border along bottom edge of cake. Arrange decorations on top of cake. Store in an airtight container. Remove decorations before serving.

Yield: about 16 servings

Gifts from the Kitchen

The homemade treats we give at Christmastime become even more enjoyable when we add a personal touch to the presentation as well. Paired with a decorated basket, a fancy candy tin, or a cross-stitched mug, our heartfelt offerings become twice as nice to give and to receive. The delicious recipes and easy crafts in this collection are guaranteed to make your gifts from the kitchen extra special.

Brandied Nuts and Honey makes a delicious topping for cake, muffins, or ice cream. A plain paper bag covered with gift wrap and adorned with an elegant bow and tag makes a festive carrier for a decorated jar of the sweet, nutty blend.

BRANDIED NUTS AND HONEY

½ cup **each** unsalted pecan halves,
   whole unsalted macadamia nuts,
   whole unsalted hazelnuts, and
   whole unsalted cashews, toasted
1 cup honey
1 tablespoon imitation brandy extract

Layer nuts in two 8-ounce jars. In a small microwave-safe bowl, combine honey and extract. Microwave on high power (100%) for 30 seconds. Pour honey mixture over nuts; screw lids on jars. Give with serving suggestions.
Yield: 2 cups
To serve: Spoon nuts over ice cream, cake, or muffins.

COVERED GIFT BAG

You will need a paper bag, wrapping paper, ribbon, spray adhesive, craft glue, hole punch, and the following items for tag: gold foil paper, white and green paper, black felt-tip calligraphy pen with medium point, and twisted cord.

1. Carefully pull bag apart at seams and spread flat. Cut a piece of wrapping paper about 1" larger on all sides than unfolded bag.
2. (**Note:** Use spray adhesive for all gluing unless otherwise indicated.) Glue right side of unfolded bag to wrong side of wrapping paper; press firmly to secure. Trim wrapping paper even with edges of bag.
3. Refold bag along previously folded lines. Use craft glue to glue bag back together. Allow to dry.
4. Place gift in bag.
5. Fold top of bag 1½" to back. Punch two holes 1" apart ½" from center top of bag. Thread ribbon through holes and tie into a bow at front of bag.
6. For tag, glue a 4" square of gold foil paper to a 4" square of white paper. Glue a 2¾" x 1⅛" piece of green paper to gold square; trim gold square to ⅛" from green paper. Use pen to write "Happy Holidays!" on a 2¾" x 1⅜" piece of white paper; glue to tag at an angle. Punch a hole in upper left corner of tag. Loop a length of cord through hole in tag and knot ends together. Hang tag on bow.

Flavorful Herbal Wine Vinegar can be sprinkled on salad, fresh vegetables, or pasta. It's also a wonderful substitute for plain vinegar in recipes. Holiday greenery and a cheery bow dress up the bottle for delivery.

HERBAL WINE VINEGAR

1 cup white vinegar
½ cup dry red wine
1 teaspoon dried rosemary leaves, crushed
½ teaspoon garlic powder

Fresh rosemary (optional)

In a 1-pint jar with a tight fitting lid, combine all ingredients. Shake until well blended. Let stand 8 hours or overnight to allow flavors to blend. If desired, transfer to a decorative bottle and place fresh rosemary in vinegar mixture. Give with serving suggestions.
Yield: about 1½ cups vinegar
To serve: Sprinkle vinegar on salad, fresh vegetables, or pasta. Flavored vinegar may also be substituted for plain vinegar in recipes.

A gift to be savored, Herb Bread is a rich wheat bread enhanced with rosemary and thyme and garnished with fresh sage. It's extra good when served with our creamy Herb Butter. To keep the wholesome bread toasty-warm (and future treats, too!), send along our clever bread warmer.

HERB BREAD

    Fresh sage leaves to decorate
 2 packages dry yeast
 ⅓ cup warm water
 5 cups bread flour
 1 cup whole-wheat flour
 2 tablespoons dried rosemary leaves,
      crushed
 1 tablespoon dried thyme leaves,
      crushed
 2½ teaspoons salt
 1½ cups warm milk
 ½ cup honey
 ¼ cup vegetable oil
    Vegetable cooking spray
 1 egg, beaten

Press fresh sage between paper towels 8 hours or overnight.

In a small bowl, dissolve yeast in water. In a large bowl, combine flours, rosemary, thyme, and salt. Add yeast mixture, milk, honey, and oil to dry ingredients. Stir until a soft dough forms. Turn onto a lightly floured surface and knead 5 minutes or until dough becomes smooth and elastic. Place in a large bowl sprayed with cooking spray, turning once to coat top of dough. Cover and let rise in a warm place (80 to 85 degrees) 1 hour or until doubled in size. Turn dough onto a lightly floured surface and punch down. Divide dough into thirds. Shape each piece of dough into a loaf and place in a greased 5 x 9-inch loaf pan. Spray tops of loaves with cooking spray, cover, and let rise in a warm place 1 hour or until doubled in size. Brush tops of loaves with egg. Arrange pressed sage on tops of loaves; brush sage with egg.

Preheat oven to 350 degrees. Bake 25 to 30 minutes or until bread sounds hollow when tapped. Transfer to a wire rack to cool completely. Store in an airtight container. Give with Herb Butter (recipe this page).
Yield: 3 loaves bread

HERB BUTTER

 1 tablespoon plus 2 teaspoons dried
      rosemary leaves, crushed
 1 tablespoon dried thyme leaves,
      crushed
 1½ teaspoons ground cardamom
 1½ cups butter, softened
 ½ cup whipping cream

In a small food processor, process rosemary, thyme, and cardamom until finely ground. In a medium bowl, cream butter until fluffy using an electric mixer. With electric mixer running, gradually add cream; beat until fluffy. Stir in herb mixture. Spoon into jars or small ramekins, cover, and store in refrigerator. Give with Herb Bread (recipe this page).
Yield: about 2½ cups butter

BREAD WARMER

You will need two 8" squares and one 8" x 12" piece of fabric for warmer, one 1¾" x 33" bias strip of fabric for binding, two 8" squares of fusible craft batting, thread to match binding fabric, and a 6" square of unglazed terra-cotta tile (available at flooring or building supply stores).

1. Follow manufacturer's instructions to fuse both batting squares to wrong side of one 8" fabric square (top).
2. For pocket on back of warmer, match wrong sides and short edges and press 8" x 12" fabric piece in half. Match raw edges of pocket fabric piece to side and bottom edges on right side of remaining 8" fabric square (back); baste pocket piece to fabric square.
3. Place top and back wrong sides together; baste all layers together.
4. For binding, press 1 end of bias strip ½" to wrong side. With wrong sides together, press strip in half lengthwise; unfold. Press long raw edges to center; refold binding. Beginning with unpressed end of binding, insert raw edges of warmer between pressed edges of binding, mitering binding at corners; pin in place. Stitching close to inner edge of binding, sew binding to warmer. Remove all visible basting threads.
5. Place tile in pocket on back of warmer.

To use warmer, preheat oven to 350 degrees. Remove tile from pocket and place in oven for 15 minutes. Use tongs to slide tile back into pocket and place warmer in a basket with warm bread. Allow tile to cool completely before handling.

This gift is sure to sweeten the season! Delectable Pudding Candy is packed with raisins, pecans, and coconut, and red and green candied cherries add Christmas flair. For an elegant presentation, our fancy candy tin features a jewel-tone padded fabric lid and lots of shiny ribbons and trim.

PUDDING CANDY

- 3 cups granulated sugar
- 1¼ cups half and half
- 2 tablespoons light corn syrup
- 2 tablespoons butter or margarine, divided
- ½ cup raisins
- ½ cup chopped pecans
- ½ cup sweetened shredded coconut
- ½ cup chopped red and green candied cherries

Butter sides of a medium heavy saucepan. Combine sugar, half and half, corn syrup, and 1 tablespoon butter in pan. Stirring constantly, cook over medium-low heat until sugar dissolves. Using a pastry brush dipped in hot water, wash down any sugar crystals on sides of pan. Attach candy thermometer to pan, making sure thermometer does not touch bottom of pan. Increase heat to medium and bring to a boil. Cook, without stirring, until syrup reaches soft ball stage (approximately 234 to 240 degrees). Test about ½ teaspoon syrup in ice water. Syrup should easily form a ball in ice water but flatten when held in your hand. Remove from heat and add remaining 1 tablespoon butter; do not stir until syrup cools to approximately 200 degrees. Using medium speed of an electric mixer, beat candy until thickened. Stir in remaining ingredients. Pour into a buttered 7 x 11-inch baking pan. Cool completely. Cut into 1-inch squares. Store in an airtight container in refrigerator.

Yield: about 5 dozen pieces candy

FANCY CANDY TIN

You will need a tin with lid, fabric to cover lid, polyester bonded batting, gold spray paint, gold ribbons and trim, a gold shank button with shank removed, florist wire, craft glue, hot glue gun, and glue sticks.

1. Spray paint tin and lid gold; allow to dry.
2. (**Note:** Use hot glue for all gluing unless otherwise indicated.) For tin, glue a wide length of ribbon around side of tin. Glue a narrow length of ribbon along center of wide ribbon.
3. For lid, use top of lid as a pattern and cut 2 pieces of batting. Use a pencil to draw around top of lid on wrong side of fabric. Cut out fabric ½" outside pencil line. At ½" intervals, clip edge of fabric to ⅛" from pencil line.

4. Center batting pieces on wrong side of fabric piece. Center lid on batting pieces. Alternating sides and pulling fabric taut, use craft glue to glue clipped edges of fabric to side of lid; allow to dry. If necessary, trim fabric just above lip at bottom edge of lid.
5. Glue trim to side of lid, covering edges of fabric.
6. For bow, form a double-loop bow from wide ribbon; wrap bow with wire at center to secure. Form a single loop from narrow ribbon; glue loop to center of bow. Glue button to center of loop. Glue bow to lid.

Here's a yummy way to spread Christmas cheer when you need several small gifts. Almond flavorings are combined with peaches and pecans to create rich, nutty Peach-Amaretto Preserves. To deliver the treats, tuck the jars in little silver baskets adorned with coordinating gift tags, ribbons, and other trims.

PEACH-AMARETTO PRESERVES

3 pounds fresh peaches (about 10 peaches), peeled, pitted, and chopped (about 4 cups) **or** 2 packages (16 ounces each) frozen peaches, thawed and chopped
6 cups granulated sugar
2 tablespoons lemon juice
1½ cups chopped pecans
½ cup amaretto
½ teaspoon almond extract
⅛ teaspoon amaretto-flavored oil (used in candy making)

In Dutch oven, combine peaches, sugar, and lemon juice. Stirring frequently, bring mixture to a boil; cook until sugar dissolves. Reduce heat to medium-low and simmer about 45 minutes or until peaches are translucent and syrup thickens. Continue to cook until syrup runs off the side of a metal spoon in a sheet. Remove from heat; skim off foam. Stir in pecans, amaretto, almond extract, and amaretto-flavored oil. Fill sterilized jars to within ¼ inch of tops. Wipe jar rims and threads. Quickly cover with lids and screw bands on tightly. Using water-bath method as directed by the USDA, process jars 15 minutes. When jars have cooled, check seals. Lids should be curved down or remain so when pressed.
Yield: about 4 pints preserves

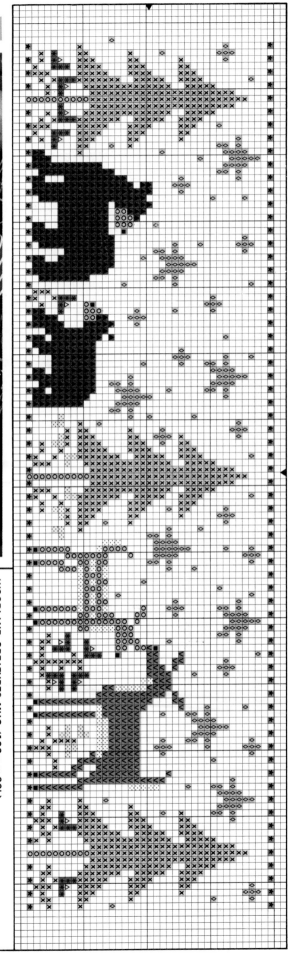

Heartwarming Tea Mix gets its refreshing appeal from a fruity blend of orange, lemon, pineapple, and coconut flavors. To complete the gift, include a mug cross stitched with a sentimental woodland scene reflecting the peace and harmony of the season.

HEARTWARMING TEA MIX

- 1 jar (15 ounces) instant orange breakfast drink mix
- 1 cup granulated sugar
- 1 cup unsweetened instant tea powder
- ½ cup presweetened lemonade-flavored soft drink mix
- 1 teaspoon **each** imitation pineapple extract and imitation coconut extract

In a blender or food processor, combine all ingredients. Give with serving instructions.
Yield: about 4¼ cups tea mix
To serve: Stir a rounded tablespoonful tea mix into 6 ounces hot water.

WOODLAND CREATURES MUG (132w x 39h)

X	DMC	JPC	COLOR
◇	ecru	1002	ecru
▨	310	8403	black
★	321	3500	red
▷	434	5000	tan
✕	436	5943	lt tan
○	562	6213	green
✔	725	2298	yellow
✱	825	7181	blue
■	838	5381	brown
▫	3731		rose
	3753		vy lt blue

Design was centered and stitched on a Vinyl-weave® (14 ct) insert from a Crafter's Pride Stitch-A-Mug™. Three strands of floss were used for Cross Stitch.

TRACING PATTERNS

When one-half of pattern (indicated by dashed line on pattern) is shown, fold tracing paper in half and place fold along dashed line of pattern. Trace pattern half, marking all placement symbols and markings; turn folded paper over and draw over all markings. Unfold pattern and lay flat. Cut out pattern.

When entire pattern is shown, place tracing paper over pattern and trace pattern, marking all placement symbols and markings. Cut out pattern.

SEWING SHAPES

1. Center pattern on wrong side of 1 fabric piece and use fabric marking pencil to draw around pattern. **DO NOT CUT OUT SHAPE.**
2. Place fabric pieces right sides together. Leaving an opening for turning, carefully sew pieces together **directly on pencil line.**
3. Leaving a ¼" seam allowance, cut out shape. Clip seam allowance at curves and corners. Turn shape right side out. Use the rounded end of a small crochet hook to completely turn small areas.

STENCILING

1. For first stencil, cut a piece of acetate 1" larger on all sides than entire pattern. Center acetate over pattern and use a permanent felt-tip pen with fine point to trace outlines of all areas of first color in stencil cutting key. For placement guidelines, outline remaining colored areas using dashed lines. Using a new piece of acetate for each color in stencil cutting key, repeat for remaining stencils.
2. Place each acetate piece on cutting mat and use craft knife to cut out stencil along solid lines, making sure edges are smooth.
3. Hold or tape first stencil in place. Use a clean dry stencil brush for each color of paint. Referring to color key, dip brush in paint and remove excess on paper towel. Brush should be almost dry to produce good results. Beginning at edge of cutout area, apply paint in a stamping motion to designated areas of design. If indicated in key, highlight or shade design by stamping a lighter or darker shade of paint in cutout area. Repeat until all areas of first stencil have been painted. Carefully remove stencil; allow paint to dry.

4. Using stencils in order indicated in stencil cutting key and matching guidelines on stencils to previously stenciled areas, repeat Step 3 for remaining stencils.

PAPIER MÂCHÉ

1. Follow manufacturer's instructions to mix instant papier mâché with water. Mixture can be stored in a resealable plastic bag in refrigerator for up to 4 days.
2. Use measurements given in project instructions as general guidelines. Keep fingers wet when working with papier mâché. Apply a ⅛" to ¼" thick layer of papier mâché over indicated shape(s). If indicated, follow project instructions to add additional details to wet papier mâché. Allow to dry completely.

CROSS STITCH

COUNTED CROSS STITCH
Work 1 Cross Stitch to correspond to each colored square in the chart. For horizontal rows, work stitches in 2 journeys (**Fig. 1**). For vertical rows, complete each stitch as shown in **Fig. 2**. When working over 2 fabric threads, work Cross Stitch as shown in **Fig. 3**. When the chart shows a Backstitch crossing a colored square (**Fig. 4**), a Cross Stitch (**Fig. 1, 2,** or **3**) should be worked first; then the Backstitch (**Fig. 7**) should be worked on top of the Cross Stitch.

Fig. 1

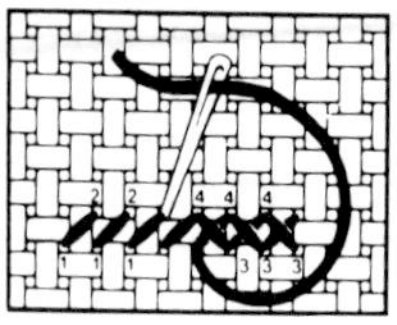

Fig. 2

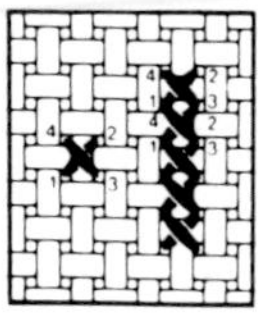

Fig. 3

Fig. 4

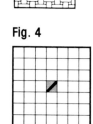

QUARTER STITCH (¼X and ¾X):
Quarter Stitches are denoted by triangular shapes of color in chart and color key. For the One-Quarter Stitch (¼X), come up at 1 (**Fig. 5**); then split fabric thread to go down at 2. When stitches 1 - 4 are worked in the same color, the resulting stitch is called a Three-Quarter Stitch (¾X). **Fig. 6** shows the technique for

Quarter Stitches when working over two fabric threads.

Fig. 5

Fig. 6

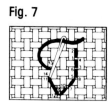
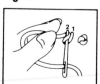

BACKSTITCH
For outline detail, Backstitch (shown in chart and color key by black or colored straight lines) should be worked after the design has been completed (**Fig. 7**).

Fig. 7

FRENCH KNOT
Bring needle up at 1. Wrap floss once around needle and insert needle at 2, holding end of floss with non-stitching fingers (**Fig. 8**). Tighten knot; then pull needle through fabric, holding floss until it must be released. For a larger knot, use more strands; wrap only once.

Fig. 8

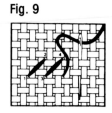

WORKING ON LINEN
Using a hoop is optional when working on linen. Roll excess fabric from left to right until stitching area is in proper position. Use the sewing method when working over 2 threads. To use the sewing method, keep your stitching hand on the right side of the fabric; take the needle down and up with 1 stroke. To add support to stitches, place the first Cross Stitch on the fabric with the stitch 1 - 2 beginning and ending where a vertical fabric thread crosses over a horizontal fabric thread (**Fig. 9**).

Fig. 9

EMBROIDERY

RUNNING STITCH
Make a series of straight stitches with stitch length equal to the space between stitches (**Fig. 1**).

Fig. 1

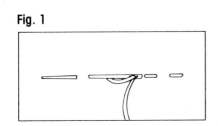

BLANKET STITCH
Referring to **Fig. 2**, come up at 1. Go down at 2 and come up at 3, keeping the thread below the point of the needle. Continue working in this manner, going down at even numbers and coming up at odd numbers (**Fig. 3**).

Fig. 2   **Fig. 3**

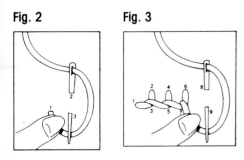

PLASTIC CANVAS

TENT STITCH
This stitch is worked over 1 intersection as shown in **Fig. 1**.

Fig. 1

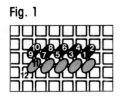

BACKSTITCH
This stitch is worked over completed stitches to outline or define (**Fig. 2**). It is sometimes worked over more than 1 thread.

Fig. 2

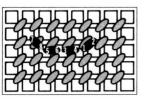

OVERCAST STITCH
This stitch covers the edge of the canvas (**Fig. 3**). It may be necessary to go through the same hole more than once to get even coverage on the edge, especially at the corners.

Fig. 3

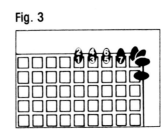

QUILTING

Thread quilting needle with an 18" length of quilting thread; knot 1 end. Bring needle up through all layers of fabric and batting; when knot catches on back of quilt, give thread a short quick pull to pop knot through backing fabric into batting (**Fig. 1**). To quilt, use small Running Stitches that are equal in length (**Fig. 2**). At the end of a length of thread, knot thread close to top fabric and take needle down through all layers of fabric and batting; when knot catches on top of quilt, pop knot through top fabric into batting. Clip thread close to fabric.

Fig. 1

Fig. 2

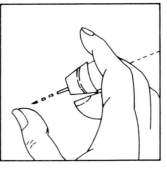

HAND APPLIQUÉ

Note: Stitches in appliqué and background fabric should be equal in length and no more than ⅛" long.

1. To appliqué shape to background fabric, bring needle up from wrong side of background fabric at 1 (**Fig. 1**). Insert needle in folded edge of appliqué at 2; bring needle out at 3 (**Fig. 2**). Insert needle into background fabric at 4; bring needle back up through background fabric at 5 (**Fig. 3**). Repeat until appliqué is secure.

Fig. 1

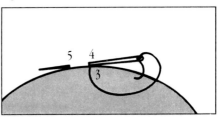

Fig. 2

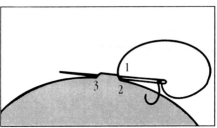

Fig. 3

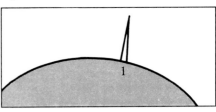

2. Knot threads on wrong side of background fabric and trim ends.

CREDITS

We wish to extend our warmest appreciation to Norma DeCamp of Norma DeCamp Designs, Hendersonville, North Carolina, and to her son, David DeCamp of Wizard's Workbench, Trappe, Maryland, for providing the exquisite Santas that appear on our cover and introductory pages.

Inspired by the legendary Father Christmases found on old Victorian cards and scraps, the DeCamp Santas are handcrafted individually. Their expressive faces, movable limbs, rich garments, and the toys and ornaments they carry in their gift pouches all contribute to their unique appearance. The hand-painted faces of these gentle gift-bringers are fashioned from a special blend of papier mâché. Their bodies and boots are carved from wood, and their splendid costumes are sewn from antique fabrics such as brocade, velvet, tapestry, fur, silk, leather, and lace. The miniature toys and ornaments they carry are made, painted, and decorated by hand. Many of these miniatures are authentic reproductions of old-fashioned Victorian playthings. For Norma and David, this attention to craftsmanship and fine details has earned them international acclaim.

The original creative force behind these Victorian Father Christmases, Norma is a self-taught folk artist who earned the nickname ''The Wizard'' when she was a little girl because of her ability to fix almost anything. Norma credits her father, who was an inventor and master machinist, with encouraging her creative bent at an early age as she worked alongside him at her own workbench in his New Hampshire shop. In addition to the Father Christmas figures pictured in our book, Norma also designs Victorian dioramas, dolls, and toys based on mythical figures, nursery rhymes, and other favorite childhood images.

Just as her father passed along his expertise and inventiveness to Norma, she has passed along her lifelong love of art to David, who spent many hours in her workshop as a child. After a formal one-year apprenticeship with his mother, David embarked on his own successful designing career. Besides the Father Christmases, David also designs elves, children, sleighs, reindeer, toys, and replicas of antique bears and rabbits. Many of David's creations are mechanical toys. Already spending many hours in his workshop, two of David's four children are following in his footsteps, ensuring that the DeCamp talent and artistry will again be passed from one generation to the next.

As a result of the public's enthusiastic response to their Victorian Santas, Norma and David have expanded what was once a fascinating hobby for each of them into two independent, successful businesses. Especially appealing to collectors, their Father Christmases have been displayed in many museums and galleries both in the United States and abroad, including the Smithsonian Institution in Washington, D.C., and the National Toy Museum in Brighton, Sussex, England.

The DeCamps' work is sold in Christmas specialty shops, antique gift shops, art galleries, interior design shops, and floral showrooms throughout the country.

We want to extend a warm thank you to the generous people who allowed us to photograph our projects in their homes.

- *Beary Merry Elves:* Marylynn and Sheffield Nelson
- *A Slice of Country Cheer:* Nancy Gunn
- *A Festival of Trees:* John and Anne Childs, and Shirley Held
- *Nutcracker Parade:* Marjorie and Bob Mathews
- *Gifts of the Magi:* Shirley Held
- *Christmas Carousel:* Sandra and Dan Cook
- *Button Country Christmas:* Nancy Gunn

To Magna IV Color Imaging of Little Rock, Arkansas, we say thank you for the superb color reproduction and excellent pre-press preparation.

We want to especially thank photographers Ken West, Larry Pennington, Mark Mathews, and Karen Shirey of Peerless Photography, Little Rock, Arkansas; and Jerry R. Davis of Jerry Davis Photography, Little Rock, Arkansas, for their time, patience, and excellent work.

To the talented people who helped in the creation of the following projects and recipes in this book, we extend a special word of thanks.

- *Flag Garland,* page 43: Nancy Spruance
- *Nutcracker Pillow,* page 56: Dick Martin
- *Carousel Horse,* page 77: Terrie Lee Steinmeyer
- *''Ho-Ho-Ho'' Sweatshirt,* page 103: Ann Townsend
- *Hearts and Bears Pinafore,* page 107: Ann Townsend
- *Snowman Tunic,* page 109: Ann Townsend
- *Santa Button Blouse,* page 110: Ann Townsend
- *Christmas Tree Sweater,* page 110: Ann Townsend
- *Woodland Creatures Mug,* page 157: Polly Carbonari
- *Crunchy Coleslaw,* page 123: Nora Faye Spencer Clift
- *Greek Pizza Squares,* page 123: E.C. Henley
- *Microwave Caramel Corn,* page 127: Ron Werle
- *Overnight Coffee Cake,* page 142: Florence Morris
- *Banana Split Dessert,* page 148: Patti Sowers

We extend a sincere thank you to all the people who assisted in making and testing the projects in this book: Jennie Black, Carrie Clifford, Trudi Drinkwater, Liz Edmonson, Margie Hill, Pat Johnson, Patricia Keightley, Pati Miller, Debra Smith, Karen Tyler, Jane Walker, and Pat Wheeler.